TRUTH IN ETHICS

Edited by

Brad Hooker

Copyright © Blackwell Publishers Ltd 1996

ISBN 0 631 19701 X

First published 1996

Blackwell Publishers
108 Cowley Road, Oxford, OX4 IJF, U.K.
and
238 Main Street,
Cambridge, MA 02142, USA.

British Library Cataloguing in Publication Data
A CIP catalogue record for this book is available from the
British Library

Library of Congress Cataloguing in Publication Data
Available from the publisher

Printed in Great Britain by Whitstable Litho, Kent
This book is printed on acid-free paper

CONTENTS

INTRODUCTION

Many distinguished philosophers have denied that moral judgements can be true. Usually, the denial was based on the idea that moral judgements are not genuine assertions of fact, but instead are expressions of sentiment or commitment. Or, as in J. L. Mackie's case, the denial started by granting that moral judgements are genuine assertions of fact, but then went on to deny that moral judgements could be true, on the grounds that the properties moral judgements ascribe do not really exist. Mackie held moral judgements to be assertions about objective reason-giving properties of things. But he denied that our metaphysics should make room for such properties. If our metaphysics eliminates such properties, and our moral judgements refer to these properties, our moral judgements cannot be true.

In the papers collected together in this volume, however, none of the authors is happy to leave the matter as Mackie left it. All are interested in the possibility of ethical judgements counting as true. But what is the proper account of ethical truth? In particular, is ethical truth integrally linked with objectivity?

Crispin Wright's paper opens the discussion by setting out his 'minimalist' account of ethical truth in terms of 'superassertability'. A statement is superassertible if it is assertible in some state of information and then remains true no matter what new information comes along. But Wright contends that the existence of truth within the realm of ethics need not be conjoined with ethical realism.

Wright thinks ethical realism — at least on one natural understanding of it — would hold that true moral judgements accurately represent or robustly correspond to moral facts that stand independent of judgements about them. What does the idea of 'robust correspondence' come to? One way of giving it substance is to say that, if true moral judgements must robustly correspond to moral facts, then moral disagreements must involve on at least one side (not only a moral but also) a rational or cognitive mistake. Another (not incompatible) way of giving it substance is to argue that moral facts play a wider role in the world than merely conferring truth-values upon moral judgements. The argument might be, for instance, that moral facts are involved in the explanation of matters in a fashion independent of anyone's making moral judgements, just as physical states and processes contribute to the explanation of things in a fashion independent of anyone's having any beliefs.

Wright thinks it is unclear what ethical realism is supposed to be, unless it is a view associated with these or closely related claims. He also thinks any such view must remain implausible. In any event, what ethical realists have fundamentally wanted, he suggests, is not that moral truth be a matter of robust correspondence, but that moral thinking intrinsically tend towards convergence. What kinds of moral appraisal offer a real possibility of convergence? Wright insists this question is one that anti-realists can be as gripped by as realists are.

In the next paper, Bernard Williams agrees with Wright that (at least some) ethical judgements can be true, and that truth in ethics does not entail ethical realism. Williams is especially interested in the question of the value of truth in ethics. In this connection, he explains how he thinks ethical truth can be related to ethical authority and knowledge.

For Williams, a crucial distinction within the realm of ethical discourse is between ethical concepts with higher empirical content, 'thick' concepts, and concepts with lower empirical content, 'thin' concepts. Examples of thick concepts are 'cruel', 'trustworthy', and 'courageous'. Examples of thin concepts are 'right', 'wrong', 'good', 'bad', 'obligatory', 'permissible'. The empirical content of thick concepts leaves less room for dispute over their application. Furthermore, here the concept of knowledge can begin to do some work. One person can be said to possess ethical knowledge if this person is better than other people at seeing what falls under a thick ethical concept.

But what about conflict between people who don't share the same thick concepts? Williams explains why he is pessimistic about the prospects of successfully recruiting everyone to share the same thick concepts. And he points out that there is little prospect of resolving ethical disputes by appealing to shared thin concepts alone: if there is going to be disagreement, shared thin concepts provide a focus for it, but not, in themselves, the means for solving it.

The paper by David Wiggins starts by explaining how objectivity links up with the notion of ethical truth. Wiggins proposes that ethics (or any other subject matter) is objective if and only if enough questions about it have answers that are simply and plainly true. Wiggins links the objective truth of a belief to the existence of a *vindicatory explanation* of that belief, that is, an explanation that precludes denying the belief's truth. Why might an explanation leave us no room to deny the truth of a belief? Because the explanation points to considerations whose cumulative force leaves us no alternative but to accept the truth of the belief, i.e., whose cumulative force leaves us, in Wiggins's terminology, 'nothing else to think'. Thus the extent to which ethical objectivism is correct depends on the extent to which there are moral considerations whose cumulative force precludes denying the truth of ethical beliefs.

Ethics is subjective, Wiggins proposes, if it is necessarily connected to conscious subjects, in particular if it is answerable only to standards set by human sentiments or responses. Wiggins catalogues a number of different ways of understanding ethics to be subjective in this sense, and points out that some of these are considerably more plausible than others. And he stresses that, if 'objective' and 'subjective' are defined as he proposes, then they are not necessarily incompatible. Morality will be both subjective and objective if it appeals to a standard founded on sentiment and if (in enough cases) the explication of that standard leaves us nothing else to think but that this or that ethical concept applies.

The second half of Wiggins's paper addresses certain points in the preceding papers of Williams and Wright. To Williams's point that some people might *decline* to think in terms of one or another ethical concept, Wiggins replies that the relevant question is whether a workable system of ethical ideas could dispense with the concept in question. If no workable system could dispense with the concept, and if the concept applies in a given case, then in the relevant sense we have nothing else to think but that it applies, and hence we have ethical objectivism. But Wiggins agrees with Williams that ethical objectivism is not to be established by *a priori* considerations about truth.

In his reply to Wright, Wiggins expresses dissatisfaction with Wright's accepting that all sorts of moral question provoke disagreements that cannot be alleviated by reference to rational or cognitive shortcomings among the parties. If this held across a whole range of moral questions, then there could be no question of truth. Wiggins also tries to cast doubt upon the clarifiability and usefulness for ethics of the contrast Wright makes between realism and anti-realism. And Wiggins draws attention to difficulties that he believes there are in Wright's notion of superassertibility.

Peter Railton's paper focuses on the question of what ethical realism might be. Railton invokes 'the seeming platitude that the nature of realism about any domain depends upon the nature of the domain itself'. Realism about physical objects construes them as having no necessary connection with human thought and feeling. But realism about human beliefs doesn't – indeed obviously couldn't – say that human beliefs have no essential connection with human subjectivity. And since realism about belief doesn't deny essential connections with human subjectivity, it can be no necessary condition of realism about a subject matter – including ethics – to deny such connections.

Railton also answers one of the most popular arguments against moral realism. This is the argument that no explanatory information would be lost if our explanations refer to moral beliefs and attitudes rather than to moral properties. Railton cites some examples where explanatory information *would* be lost if our explanations avoided reference to moral properties. Of course, anti-realists will deny that explanations need refer to moral properties. But Railton points out that here anti-realism comes at a high price. For to accept that explanations need never refer to moral properties will require extensive revision to common-sense moral theorising.

A central issue in the papers by Wright, Wiggins, and Williams is whether truth in ethics requires that moral thinking tend towards convergence. An issue especially prominent in the essays by Wright, Wiggins, and Railton is how moral truth hooks up with human subjectivity. Both of these issues are taken up in Michael Smith's paper.

Smith begins by spelling out an independent internalist requirement on moral judgement. Internalists hold that there is a necessary connection of sorts between sincerely judging an act to be right and being motivated accordingly. He then proceeds by arguing that there is an inherent instability in the different theories of moral judgement that attempt to underwrite internalism. Those that attempt to underwrite it by denying there is any such thing as truth in ethics give way to theories that embrace the idea of ethical truth, but then deny a convergence in ethical thought is required for such truth. These theories, in their turn, give way to theories that embrace the ideas of ethical truth and of convergence, but then disagree about the role of ethical facts in explaining such convergence.

Though Smith worries about the prospects of finding a theory that can both explain the internalism requirement on moral judgement and the convergence of ethical thought, he argues that one theory does a better job than the rest. The theory he defends is the non-relative version of the dispositional theory of value. This theory holds that all our moral judgements presuppose in effect that we would converge on one set of pro- and con-attitudes if we each developed a maximally coherent and rational set of such attitudes. For example, the moral judgement that we ought to give to charity in certain circumstances presupposes that, if we each came up with a maximally coherent and rational set of pro- and con-attitudes, we would converge upon a pro-attitude towards giving to charity in those circumstances.

Must all maximally coherent and rational sets of moral attitudes really converge? They may, Smith proposes, if neither the concept of maximal coherence and rationality, on the one hand, nor the concept of moral obligation, on the other, can be understood wholly independently of the other. Rather, our account of maximal coherence and rationality and our account of moral obligation must be interconnected. Here at least, the line between conceptual analysis and normative moral theorizing is blurred. On Smith's theory, the very intelligibility of ethical judgement turns on the question of how compelling the best normative moral arguments are.

All the essays in this collection record important and engaging reflections on matters of unending philosophical interest. The depth and the richness of the essays are such that no one could fail to learn from studying them. For this I am very grateful to the contributors. I am especially grateful to Bernard Williams, who chose the focus for a RATIO conference out of which this collection evolved. I am also grateful to my colleague John Cottingham for making this collection possible, and to Claire Andrews, Claire Lloyd, Steve Smith, and Richard Fidczuk of Blackwell Publishers for their help.

I

TRUTH IN ETHICS[1]

Crispin Wright

I

The tradition of anti-realist thought about ethics – manifest in the desire to make some sort of disadvantageous comparison, in point of its objectivity or the reality of the states of affairs with which it deals, between moral discourse and, say, the discourses of mathematics and physical science – is no doubt as old as moral philosophy itself. In modern times the anti-realist tendency has typically cast itself as a denial that moral statements are *true*. And this denial has in turn taken two quite different shapes. Some, like John Mackie,[2] have been willing to grant that moral discourse has all the semantical features necessary to aim at truth – that it trades in genuine assertions, apt to be true or false as literally construed – but have gone on to contend that it sweepingly and systematically fails in that aim. It does so because the truth of its statements would call for items of a metaphysically outlandish sort – queer, intrinsically reason-giving properties, for which our best science can find no explanatory use and which seem to promise no hope of reduction to the properties it does use. But this view contrasts sharply with an idea of Hume, befriended by A. J. Ayer and R. M. Hare and more recently developed by Simon Blackburn and Alan Gibbard,[3] that although moral discourse wears a surface of assertoric content, its *deep* syntax is different – that it provides a

---

[1] This paper is a lightly edited version of what I actually presented at the Reading Conference of the same name. Readers of my *Truth and Objectivity* (Cambridge, MA: Harvard University Press, 1992) may experience what Quine once called a sense of *deja lu*, for the paper is in essentials merely a collation of some of the thoughts about ethics that featured in that book along the way.

[2] J. L. Mackie, *Ethics: Inventing Right and Wrong* (Harmondsworth: Penguin, 1977).

[3] The *loci classici* of modern ethical expressivism are of course the famous 'Critique of Ethics and Theology' offered in ch. 6 of Ayer's *Language, Truth and Logic* (London: Victor Gollancz, 1936); and R. M. Hare's *The Language of Morals* (Oxford: Oxford University Press, 1952). An invaluable précis of Hare's current views is provided by his 'Universal Prescriptivism', ch. 40 of P. Singer (ed.), *A Companion to Ethics* (Oxford: Basil Blackwell, 1991). Ch. 6, 'Evaluations, Projections and Quasi-realism', of Blackburn's *Spreading the Word* (Oxford: Oxford University Press, 1984) remains the best introduction to his view; A. Gibbard's ideas are developed systematically in his *Wise Choices, Apt Feelings* (Cambridge, MA: Harvard University Press, 1990).

medium not for the depiction of facts but rather for the expression of *attitudes*. According to this expressivist form of moral anti-realism, both moral realism and its error-theoretic opposition are guilty of a mistake comparable to the assumption of a truth condition for an indicative sentence which is actually being used to express a rule, or an order.

That these tendencies have had distinguished adherents and are of long standing ought not to blind us to how unlikely it is that either can serve a satisfactory moral philosophy. The Mackie view allows that a moral thinker quests for truth, and uses a discourse which, at least as far as its semantics is concerned, is fitted to that project. But the world lets the moral thinker down; there are no real moral properties out there, no moral facts. The great discomfort with such a view is that, unless more is said, it simply relegates moral discourse to bad faith. Whatever we may once have thought, as soon as philosophy has taught us that the world is unsuited to confer truth on any of our claims about what is right, or wrong, or obligatory, etc., the reasonable response ought surely to be to forgo making any such claims. That wouldn't be to forgo the right to any form of moral sentiment, I suppose. But it would, apparently, be to forgo any conception of a *proper basis* for such sentiment – to forgo the point of reasoned appreciation and debate about what is moral, and of criticism of others' opinions about it. Such consequences are surely calamitous. If it is of the essence of moral judgement to aim at the truth, and if philosophy teaches us that there is no moral truth to hit, how are we supposed to take ourselves seriously in thinking the way we do about any issue which we regard as of major moral importance? How can opinions which cool philo-sophical reflection teaches are no better than superstition be rationally permitted to constrain one's actions in the way that moral opinions distinctively do?

One form of response to this kind of difficulty which has found favour with error-theorists generally is to seek to disclose some other purpose for the discourse in question, some norm of appraisal *besides* truth, at which its statements can be seen as aimed, and which they can satisfy. Hartry Field's[4] nominalist play with the idea of *conservativeness* in pure mathematics precisely represents an attempt at such a strategy: in Field's view, pure mathematical statements are typically literally false – since their truth would call

---

[4] H. Field, *Science Without Numbers* (Oxford: Basil Blackwell, 1980), and *Realism, Mathematics and Modality* (Oxford: Basil Blackwell, 1989).

for metaphysically outlandish objects of various kinds – but we may rationally endorse them nevertheless because their falsity does not compromise their *inferential utility*: when adjoined to metaphysically pukka, non-outlandish statements of whatever sort, they allow for the derivation only of consequences that independently follow from those statements (which makes them harmless), and typically greatly facilitate the construction of such derivations (which makes them useful).

But this strategy invites what seems to me a very good question: if, among the welter of falsehoods which we enunciate in moral discourse, there is a good distinction to be drawn between those which are acceptable in the light of some such subsidiary norm and those which are not – a distinction which actually informs ordinary discussion and criticism of moral claims – then why insist on construing *truth* for moral discourse in terms which motivate a charge of global error, rather than explicate it in terms of the satisfaction of the putative subsidiary norm, whatever it is? The question may have a good answer. The error-theorist may be able to argue that the superstition that he finds in ordinary moral thought goes too deep to permit any construction of moral truth which avoids it to be acceptable as an account of *moral* truth. But I do not know of promising argument in that direction.

The prospects for a satisfying moral expressivism seem to me to be equally doubtful. Moral discourse is *disciplined* to a very great degree. Acceptable moral opinion is not just a matter of what feels comfortable, but has to survive appraisal by quite refined and complicated standards. Moral argument can be difficult, and its conclusions unobvious. But to whatever extent such generally acknowledged underlying standards inform the appraisal of particular moral judgements and argument, to that extent the claim that moral discourse is not genuinely assertoric but serves merely as a medium for the expression of attitude will seem unmotivated in contradistinction to the idea that the truth predicate which applies within it is some sort of construct out of the relevant species of discipline. And the force of this complaint is greatly enhanced (so it seems to me, though I do not pretend to a command of all the most recent expressivist manoeuvres) by the fact that we do not seem yet to have been provided with any clear and workable idea of how to construe discourses which exhibit all the overt syntactic trappings of assertion – negation, the conditional construction, embedding within propositional attitudes, hypothesis and inference and so on – in such a way that the contents involved are not assertoric but are presented with illocutionary force of quite a different kind, apt to the expression of attitude.

It's worth briefly illustrating this with reference to a well-known proposal of Simon Blackburn's.[5] Consider the following sample argument:

> *Premise* 1 Stealing is wrong.
> *Premise* 2 If stealing is wrong, conniving at stealing is wrong.
> ∴ *Conclusion* Conniving at stealing is wrong.

This is a moral *modus ponens* – a very simple, valid piece of moral reasoning. What account can the expressivist offer of its validity? Well, if moral statements are not strictly speaking assertions, then the major premise 2 cannot be an assertion either – you cannot make an assertion by yoking together non-assertions with a binary connective; indeed the ordinary conditional cannot be so much as grammatically applied to an antecedent that is not assertoric. So what is the logical form of premise 2? All the expressivist can offer, it seems, is that it is the expression of a complex attitude – a *conditional* attitude: roughly, to affirm 2 is to endorse taking a negative moral attitude towards conniving at stealing if a negative moral attitude is taken towards stealing itself.

Now the striking effect of this – essentially Blackburn's – construal of the content of the two premises is that there will be at the worst a *moral* failing on the part of one who accepts them but fails to possess the attitude which would be expressed by an endorsement of the conclusion. If I disapprove of stealing, and applaud disapproval of conniving on the part of anyone who disapproves of stealing, yet do not myself disapprove of conniving, then I merely fail to have an attitude of which, were I to have it, I would, in the circumstances, approve. I fail to live up to my values, if you like. That is a lapse; but it is not the grotesque lapse of rationality that ought to be involved in a failure to accept the stated conclusion on the part of one who accepts the premises 1 and 2. If the expressivist doesn't have the resources to find the more grotesque, rational failing, that's a sure sign there's something wrong with the account.

Expressivists, including Blackburn, have had other proposals to make about this particular type of difficulty, of course. But one inclined to an intuitive anti-realism about morals – to the kind of disadvantageous comparison that I mentioned – ought to worry

---

[5] See *Spreading the Word*, ch. 6.

about a direction of development of his basic intuition which holds out so substantial a hostage to syntactico-reconstructive fortune. And if expressivism grinds to a stop on this type of difficulty, can it really be that only error-theory – the classification of morality as superstition – can provide a vehicle for the anti-realist?

That will certainly be the situation if to concede truth to moral statements is to concede realism. In that case the only anti-realist options must involve the denial of truth, either because moral statements are not so much as truth-apt or because, though truth-apt, they are largely false. But what we want, of course, is a way of casting the anti-realist intuition which is consistent with the integrity of moral discourse and argument, and which allows us to take a moral point of view with a clean intellectual conscience. Conversely, it doesn't seem as though the failings of error-theory and expressivism should count as establishing realism by elimination. So there had better be another shape for ethical anti-realism to take. But what shape?

II

Here is one proposal. We need to win through to a conception of truth which allows us to grant truth-aptitude, and indeed truth, to responsible judgements within a given discourse without thereby conceding a realist view of it. Such a view will hold that to ascribe truth to a statement need not be to ascribe a property of intrinsic metaphysical *gravitas*, that any sentence is a candidate for truth which is possessed of assertoric content, and that possession of assertoric content is essentially a matter of meeting certain syntactic and disciplinary constraints – essentially, sentences are assertoric which are capable of significant embedding within constructions such as negation, the conditional, and in contexts of propositional attitude, and whose use is subject to acknowledged standards of warrant. When such standards are satisfied that will then suffice, other things being equal, defeasibly to justify the claim that the sentence in question is true.

Now there is, of course, on the market a long-standing conception of truth which accomplishes all this – the so-called *deflationary* conception, according to which 'true' may indeed significantly be predicated of all sentences in the catchment just outlined, without heavyweight metaphysical commitment, precisely because the word does not express a real property at all but is only a device of *endorsement*, a device we need only because we sometimes want to endorse a statement given by a noun phrase, like 'Riemann's Hypothesis' or 'what he just said', which does not specify its content, or because we want to endorse whole batches of statements at once ('Most of what he said is true'). But the deflationary conception will not serve our present purpose. I have argued elsewhere[6] that to accept that a truth predicate can be defined upon any discourse which counts as assertoric in the sense we are concerned with, and to accept that any such predicate must be governed by the Disquotational Scheme:

'p' is true if and only if p,

enforces the recognition (i) that the word 'true' will record a norm governing assertion and belief-formation which is distinct from assertibility, i.e. warrant by whatever standards inform the discourse in question, and (ii) that its compliance or non-compliance with *this* norm can hardly fail to be reckoned to be a substantial property of a statement. I won't rehearse the considerations that drive that conclusion now. What I want to dwell on for a minute is how it might be possible for the anti-realist to grant that moral discourse may be truth apt, and to allow – as the error-theorist cannot – that ordinary good grounds for a particular moral opinion are indeed grounds for taking it to be true, while retaining room for conceiving of truth as a substantial property, and so avoiding deflationism.

Consider a parallel with the concept of identity. In one sense the notion of identity is invariant as we consider different ranges of individuals. Its invariance is sustained by uniform inferential links, grounded in the twin platitudes that everything is self-identical and that identicals share all their properties. Nevertheless what *constitutes* identity is subject to considerable variation as we vary the kind of objects with which we are concerned. Thus the identity of material objects is arguably constituted by spatio-temporal continuity; identity and distinctness among numbers, on the other hand, according to Frege's famous account, are dictated by relations of one-one correspondence among associated concepts; the shapes of plane figures are identified and distinguished by relations of geometrical similarity among them; identity among directions of lines is constituted by relations of parallelism between lines; and it is notoriously elusive what constitutes identity for

---

[6] See *Truth and Objectivity*, ch. 1, § III.

persons, though considerations of bodily and psychological continuity call the shots.

The notion of 'constitution' here invoked could no doubt be usefully clarified, but I see no reason to question the authenticity of the general idea that the instantiation of a certain concept may be constituted in different ways, depending on the kind of instantiators concerned. So: identity is one concept, but what constitutes the identity of a with b may vary, depending on the type of individual a and b are. Evidently there is space for a corresponding contention about truth. There need be no single, discourse-invariant thing in which truth consists. Depending on the type of statement with which we are concerned, the constitution of truth may sometimes reside in factors congenial to an intuitive realism, sometimes not.

I should emphasise, lest there be any misunderstanding, that the pluralism I am canvassing would not involve the idea that 'true' is ambiguous, any more than a corresponding conclusion is invited about 'is identical to'. An ambiguous term typically needs a variety of explanations, each determining a different extension for it. But if we can make out the parallel with identity, we will succeed in disclosing a basic set of principles – corresponding to the reflexivity and unrestricted congruence of identity – which will govern the concept of truth in all areas of discourse. These principles will enshrine all that can be said in general about the explanation of the word, and to that extent its meaning will be uniform. Moreover one such principle will certainly be the Disquotational Scheme, which will ensure that any pair of predicates each of which qualifies as a truth predicate for a given discourse will have to coincide in extension. 'True', therefore, cannot be ambiguous as are 'stage', 'still', and 'rush'.

What might be the principles which such a view of truth could call upon to play the analogous role to reflexivity and unrestricted congruence in the case of identity? Well, a place should certainly be found for the Disquotational Scheme, on which traditional deflationism more or less exclusively focuses. But lurking behind the Disquotational Scheme is the more fundamental thesis that to assert is to present as true. Other relevant principles would be:

that to every truth-apt content corresponds a truth-apt negation;

that a content is true just in case it corresponds to the facts, depicts things as they are, and so on;

that truth and justification are distinct;

that truth is absolute – there is no being more or less true;

that truth is stable – if a content is ever true, it always is.

Arguable further additions would concern the connections between truth and transformations of tense and other indexicals, and principles concerning other connectives besides negation. The controlling thought remains that to be a truth predicate is merely to satisfy a set of very general, very intuitive a priori laws – in effect, the platitudes noted and their kin.

Investigation discloses that any discourse which is assertoric in the sense we are concerned with – a discourse meeting the basic disciplinary and syntactic constraints outlined – will allow the definition upon it of a predicate which satisfies all these platitudes about truth.[7] Since, according to the view proposed, there is no more to an expression's being a truth predicate than its satisfaction of those platitudes, there will accordingly be no room left for the expressivist view that, appearances to the contrary, such a discourse does not really deal in truth-apt contents.[8] Equally, since the Disquotational Scheme will control the truth predicate in question, reason to accept any statement of the discourse in question will be reason to regard it as true, and there will be no space for the sort of metaphysical rift between truth and justification by ordinary standards which is the error-theorist's stock-in-trade.

III

That, then, is the outline of an approach that might provide what we want – a perspective on truth and truth-aptitude which will allow the moral anti-realist to grant that moral discourse enjoys both without jettison of the idea that truth is a real property. But I have merely sketched a shape. What needs to be indicated now,

[7] For synopsis of the relevant considerations, see *Truth and Objectivity*, ch. 2, § I, and ch. 3, § I.

[8] This claim has proved to seem too swift to some, who have urged that it should be consistent with a discourse's sustaining a predicate which satisfies all the platitudes noted that it fail to provide a medium for the expression of *belief* – conceived, à la Hume, as, unlike both desire and e.g. ethical attitude, an intrinsically unmotivational state. Since it is plausibly also a platitude that beliefs are what sincere assertions express, it would follow that the assertoric character of moral discourse in particular is not so easily secured. The issue is usefully debated in the contributions by M. Smith (twice), J. Divers and A. Miller, and P. Horwich to the symposium on 'Expressivism and Truth' in *Analysis* 54 (1994), pp. 1–26. The objection is also pressed by F. Jackson in his review of *Truth and Objectivity* in *Philosophical Books* 35 (1994), pp. 162–9. I respond in the same number of that journal, pp. 169–75.

pursuing the analogy with identity, are counterparts of the ways in which identity can be variously constituted among varying kinds of identicals, some ways of being true being more, and some less congenial to intuitive realist and anti-realist inclination.

Consider any type of opinion for which we feel we can pretend to no conception of how truth might lie beyond human recognition in principle. Opinion about what is and isn't funny would seem to provide one example. Disagreement in such opinions may of course be intractable in principle, but in such a case we shall hesitate to regard either conflicting opinion as true. What seems to make no sense is the idea of a situation being determinate in comic quality, as it were, although human beings are simply not empowered, even in principle, to recognise that quality. By contrast, many would be comfortable with the idea that in some areas of enquiry the connection between prosecution of best method and getting at the truth is, at bottom, 'serendipitous', so that, for example, the internally blameless prosecution of best scientific method by theorists with somewhat different starting points may lead to the generation of incompatible but rationally incommensurable scientific theories.

Some forms of realist construal of the content of moral judgements – those which see moral truth as grounded in the will of God, for example, or as a potentially incalculable function of social utility – would have the effect of placing morality in the latter camp. But many would feel that there is little, if any, more sense than in the case of comedy to be given to the idea that moral quality may in principle outreach the efforts of an ordinarily receptive, careful moral thinker. Now one very important consideration – which needs detailed substantiation I can't provide now – is that when a region of thought has that feature, viz. that no clear sense can be attached to the idea that it provides means for the expression of truths which human beings are constitutionally incapable of recognising, then the concept I have elsewhere given the somewhat ungainly title of *superassertibility* will effectively function as a truth predicate: that is, superassertibility will validate the basic platitudes about truth which, according to the approach I have outlined, are constitutive of the notion.[9]

Superassertibility, as the term suggests, is a construction out of ordinary assertibility. Ordinary assertibility is relative to a state of information: it is as assessed in a particular informational

---

[9] See *Truth and Objectivity*, ch. 2, §§ V and, more especially, VI.

context that statements are or are not assertible. Superassertibility, by contrast, is an absolute notion: a statement is superassertible if it is assertible in some state of information and then remains so no matter how that state of information is enlarged upon or improved.

It is instructive to compare superassertibility with the conception of truth, also constructed out of assertibility, favoured by some of the American pragmatists. C. S. Peirce conceived of truth as what is assertible – justified – at some ideal limit of enquiry, when all relevant information is in. Superassertibility, by contrast, avoids play with arguably mythical limits: it is a matter of enduring assertibility under an ideally prosecuted, indefinitely continuing investigation, rather than of assertibility attained when such an investigation is somehow completed.

I suspect that some, though probably not all, of the criticisms frequently levelled at the claims of the Peircian notion to amount to a concept of truth could have been deflected if pragmatists had worked with superassertibility instead. But however that may be, it should be clear that any assertoric discourse, disciplined by acknowledged standards of acceptability for its statements, must allow the definition on the back of those standards of a species of superassertibility: it will be a matter of justification in the light of those standards in a particular context, and of the survival of that justification no matter how much additional relevant information is accrued. There is therefore the option, for those who are content to think of morals as analogous to comedy in the relevant respect, of thinking of moral truth as a kind of superassertibility: the morally true is that which can be morally justified and which then retains that justification no matter how refined or extensive an additional consideration is given to the matter.

Moral superassertibility, so described, is vague and highly abstract. But the important thing about it comes across even at this level of characterisation. It is that it is a *language-game internal* notion, as it were. Superassertibility is a projection of whatever internal discipline informs a discourse (and such discipline there has to be if we are dealing in genuine contents). To think of a discourse as dealing with truth-apt contents, accordingly, need involve, when truth is conceived as superassertibility, no work for a type of idea which is absolutely central to traditional realist thinking: the idea of *correspondence*, of representation of real, external states of affairs. When truth is so conceived, various relations between truth and superassertibility will be possible. The superassertibility of a statement may be *explained* by its being true (if our standards of acceptability track the truth) or the two concepts may diverge in extension (if they do not). But there will be no *identity*. One basic form of opposition between realist and anti-realist views of a discourse will be between those who think of the truth of a statement as constituted in some substantial relation of fit or representation – the traditional imagery of the mirror – and those who conceive, or might as well conceive, of truth as superassertibility, as durable satisfaction of the discourse's internal disciplinary constraints.

Before developing that a little, let me pause to note how the looseness of the notion of moral superassertibility, as so far characterised, immediately allows an important fragmentation within the anti-realist camp. Moral truth, for the anti-realist, will be durable justifiability in the light of the standards that discipline ordinary moral thinking. But which standards are those? There is nothing in the proposal to pre-empt all belief in moral progress – belief in the possibility of a gradual refinement of moral thinking and of a gradual convergence in moral points of view, stabilised by the standards that are the very products of that refinement. But that optimistic conception contrasts with two possible others. Some will be tempted to view the detail of the discipline to which moral thinking is subjected as essentially *local* – to a culture, or a nation, or a period, or an age-group – and will want to deny that moral thinking embodies any intrinsic dynamic towards convergence across widely differing standpoints. The discipline is real enough, on this view, but it is essentially a parochial form of discipline and it is merely a sociological question how far the parish can be made to extend. Finally, and less optimistic still, there is space for the *irrealist* or nihilist view that the whole notion of the discipline to which moral discourse is subject is a sort of charade, an illusion comparable to that which, in Wittgenstein's view, conditions the idea that there could be a language fit for the description of sensations conceived as Cartesian private objects. (Such a view of morals seems evidently to fly in the face of the social facts. I mention it only to indicate how the general map of the issues which I'm proposing does leave a corner for the irrealist to try to occupy.)

Reverting to the issue of realism, there may seem to be a tension between the suggestion that the hallmark of a realist conception of truth is its implication of the notion of representation, or fit, and the inclusion, among the set of basic platitudes constitutive of any truth predicate, of one to the effect that to be true is to correspond to the facts. It is crucial to see that this is not really a difficulty. It is indeed a platitude that a statement is true if and only if it corresponds to the facts. But it is so only in so far as we understand a statement's correspondence to fact to involve no more than that matters stand as it affirms. For reflect that if 'p' says that p, then matters will stand as 'p' affirms if and only if p. Since by the Disquotational Scheme, 'p' is true if and only if p, it follows that matters stand as 'p' affirms just in case 'p' is true – essentially the Correspondence Platitude. What this simple argument brings out, however, is not that there is no alternative to a realist conception of truth – that realism is built into the core of the notion – but rather that the phraseology of correspondence may embody much less of a metaphysical commitment than realism supposes. Correspondence phraseology – and all the paraphrases of it that we are likely to think of – are co-licensed, as it were, with talk of truth. But since, as just illustrated, the Correspondence Platitude is a *derived* platitude, it follows that such talk need have no more content than flows into it, so to speak, from the parent platitudes that license that derivation. On the surface, the Correspondence Platitude takes us from a predicate, 'true', to a relation, and lays it down as necessary and sufficient for the predicate to apply to a statement that the latter bears that relation to a suitably designated object-term. I suggest that the question for the realist has to be whether our understanding of what it is for this relation to obtain has, in the case of any particular discourse, *more* to it than can be derived from the co-permissibility of the claim that it obtains with the claim that a relevant statement is true, and the co-permissibility of the latter with the claim that the statement is assertible. *That* much understanding is what is bestowed by the derivability of the Correspondence Platitude from the minimal platitudes concerning any truth predicate. The realist – one who holds to a contrast between a representational conception of truth, so to say, and superassertibility, and maintains that it is the former which operates in a favoured region of discourse – owes us some additional substance to his talk of 'representation', 'correspondence', and 'facts', which the Correspondence Platitude, as a mere platitude, is insufficient to ensure.

Naturally, there can only be two places to look for such additional substance. One is the relational term – the idea of representation, or correspondence. Here the quest will be for some additional aspect to our understanding of the relational term, exceeding anything imposed by its liaison with the minimal platitudes, which somehow gives a point to realist intuition in the area of discourse in question. The other course is to work on the object term – *the facts* – and, once again, to try to show how we are committed, in that area, to a more robust conception of them than is entrained merely by the ubiquitous permission to gloss 'is true' as 'corresponds to the facts'.

In the space I have remaining, I'll try rapidly to indicate how some quite familiar considerations from the debates concerning moral realism slot neatly into this perspective, tending to show – if they are correct – that the would-be moral realist cannot live up to the demands of the kind of robustly representational conception of truth by which I am proposing that realism generally should define itself. Then in conclusion I'll offer some brief, necessarily inadequate reflections about why, as it seems to me at least, the failure of moral realism would not have to be a matter of concern.

IV

The thought of a realist – unless he is pessimistic enough to think that what is true in the relevant region of discourse is altogether beyond our ken – is that responsibly to practise in that region is to enter into a kind of representational mode of cognitive function, comparable in relevant respects to, say, taking a photograph or making a wax impression of a key. Certain matters stand thus and so independently of us (compare the photographed scene and the contours of the key). We engage in a certain process, to wit, we put ourselves at the mercy, so to speak, of the standards of appraisal appropriate to the discourse in question (compare taking the snapshot or impressing the key on the wax). And the result is to leave an imprint in our minds which, in the best case, appropriately matches the independently standing state of affairs.

Philosophers, most notably the early Wittgenstein and J. L. Austin,[10] have of course tried to be much more definite about this type of conception. But even vaguely so presented, it does have certain quite definite obligations. If we take photographs of the *same* scene which somehow turn out to represent it in incompatible ways, there has to have been some kind of shortcoming in the function of one of the cameras, or in the way it was used. If the wax

---

[10] The *locus classicus* for Austin's view, of course, is his 'Truth', originally in the *Proceedings of the Aristotelian Society* suppl. vol. 24 (1950), and reprinted in his collected *Philosophical Papers*, edited by J. O. Urmson and G. J. Warnock (Oxford: Oxford University Press, 2nd edition 1970).

impressions we take of a single key turn out to be of such a shape that no one key can fit them both, then again there has to have been some fault in the way we went about it, or in the materials used. The price you pay for taking the idea of representation in the serious way the realist wants to take it is that when subjects' representations prove to conflict, then (prescinding from certain necessary qualifications, mainly to do with vagueness, which I won't elaborate now) there has to have been something amiss with the way they were arrived at or with their vehicle – the wax, the camera, or the thinker. Accordingly, one obligation of the moral realist will be to hold, and therefore to justify holding, that moral disagreements, since they involve a clash of what purport to be substantial representations, have to involve defects of process or materials: at least one of the protagonists has to be guilty of a deficiency in the way he arrives at his view, or to be somehow constitutionally unfit.

That is an obligation imposed by an attempt to imbue the notion of representation, or correspondence, with a more full-blooded content than it derives from the Correspondence Platitude. The second obligation derives from the correlative attempt to find additional substance in 'the facts' to which true statements correspond. Broadly, it ought to be possible to justify conceiving of such facts as just as robust and independent of the practice of the discourse in which we supposedly aim to represent them as are the photographed scene and the impressed key. What would that involve?

What needs to be shown is that the relevant beliefs are exactly an *epiphenomenon* – that they are, as it were, driven by the facts. And it is hard to see how that might be shown except by showing how the primary phenomena – the states of affairs such beliefs allegedly represent – display other forms of impact upon and interaction within the wider world than are involved in their connections with the epiphenomena. It is unclear how to think about the matter except along these broad lines.

The second obligation on the realist is therefore exactly the dual of an alleged obligation that an influential recent debate – I'm thinking of that involving Harman, Wiggins and the so-called Cornell Realists[11] – has pivoted around. That debate involves a

---

[11] See G. Harman, *The Nature of Morality* (New York: Oxford University Press, 1977). Ch. 1 is reprinted as 'Ethics and Observation' in G. Sayre-McCord (ed.), *Essays on Moral Realism* (Ithaca NY: Cornell University Press, 1988). David Wiggins's principal contributions to the debate are Essay IV of his *Needs, Values, Truth* (Oxford: Basil Blackwell, 1987), p. 156, and

challenge to the realist to explain how moral states of affairs
contribute to the best explanation of moral beliefs. What I am
urging that the realist had better be able to do, by contrast, is to
explain how moral states of affairs contribute to the explanation of
things *other than* moral beliefs.

Of course, the two areas of obligation need more refined
presentation and discussion. But enough has maybe been said to
indicate why the ante-post betting might favour the anti-realist. As
far as the first obligation is concerned, it is of course evident that
moral disagreements can be and frequently are attributable to
confused thinking, factual ignorance, and sheer prejudice. But the
obligation imposed by a robust reading of the notion of representation is to show that deficiency *has* to be involved in the generation of
any such dispute (prescinding from the irrelevant case of vagueness). Any student of morality who has come to feel, therefore, that
a substantial body of the principles that inform our ordinary moral
thought are essentially contestable, and that no rational or
cognitive deficiency is needed to sustain the clashes on things like
sexual morality, the value of individual freedom, the moral status of
animals, and the ethics of suicide and mercy-killing, which are
freely exemplified within and across cultures, won't give much for
the realist's chances.

As far as the second obligation is concerned, we have to ask: of
the obtaining of what states of affairs might the obtaining of moral
states of affairs contribute towards the explanation? Much of the
detail of the debate about the best explanation of moral belief to
which I alluded is of course relevant to this question. But without
going into that, it is difficult to see that matters can in the end turn
out very satisfactorily from a realist point of view. What is there
that is so strictly because such-and-such a *moral* state of affairs
obtains – a state of affairs, say, of the general form: such-and-such
circumstances impose such-and-such an obligation upon an agent
who meets certain conditions?

By way of comparison consider the state of affairs of a pond's
being frozen over. Reference to the ice-covering on the pond can

his 'Moral Cognitivism, Moral Relativism and Motivating Moral Beliefs', in *Proceedings of the Aristotelian Society* 91 (1990–1). The leading 'Cornell Realist' is Nicholas Sturgeon. See in particular his 'Moral Explanations' in D. Copp and D. Zimmerman (eds.), *Morality, Reason and Truth* (Totowa, NJ: Rowman and Allenheld, 1985). Sturgeon's debate with Harman is continued in a further exchange in N. Gillespie (ed.), *Moral Realism: Proceedings of the 1985 Spindel Conference, Southern Journal of Philosophy* suppl. vol. 24 (1986).

contribute towards explaining at least four distinct kinds of thing:

(a) someone's perceiving, and hence believing, that the pond is frozen;
(b) the tendency of the goldfish to cluster towards the bottom of the pond;
(c) someone's slipping and falling when stepping onto the surface;
(d) the tendency of a Celsius thermometer to read zero when placed on the surface.

The ice-covering on the pond can be ascribed, that is, each of four kinds of consequence: cognitive effects; effects on sentient, but non-conceptual creatures; effects on us as physically interactive agents; and certain brute effects on inanimate matter. By contrast, although some philosophers have made a case that moral facts can contribute towards the explanation of agents' moral beliefs, the kind of fact about obligation cited would seem unfitted to play any part in the *direct* – that is, propositional-attitude -unmediated – explanation of any effects of the latter three sorts: it is hard to think of anything which is true of sentient but non-conceptual creatures, or of mobile organisms, or of inanimate matter, which is true because such a moral fact obtains and in whose explanation it is unnecessary to advert to anyone's appreciation of that moral fact.[12]

V

Naturally, these reflections ought to leave a realist unmoved who conceives that morality is backed by some sort of external sanction, either on traditional theological lines or because some naturalistic reconstruction of moral fact is proposed. But it seems to me that there would some unclarity at this point about the motives of a moral realist who, as a way of maintaining the line, proposed to *seek* some such reconstruction. For what should a sensible moral realist want which cannot be incorporated in the kind of anti-realism which, viewing truth as a real property, grants the truth-aptitude of moral discourse, and allows that responsible moral opinion may justifiably claim to be true?

---

[12] The limitation gestured at here is meant to be *a priori*: it is not that moral facts are merely accidentally lazy, as it were. Accidental laziness would not be enough to create a tension with the robustness of moral facts.

Such an anti-realism discounts any suggestion that moral discourse is beset by systematic error, or is merely the sheepish expression of emotion masked by the wolfish syntax of genuine judgement. As earlier noted, it can also be hospitable, merely *qua* anti-realism, to the idea that the sensibilities on which moral discourse is founded are capable of *improvement* – that morals can undergo significant development and, by dint of our efforts, the story of our moral development can unfold better than it might otherwise have done. It is true the anti-realist will have to grant that such ideas of progress or deterioration are ones which we can have use for only from *within* a committed moral point of view; that any refinement of which our moral sensibilities are capable can only be a matter of the approaching of a certain equilibrium as appraised by the exercise of those very sensibilities. And making out that there is indeed such a dynamic towards equilibrium in moral thought will need a lot of sensitive work. But suppose that project cannot succeed, and our moral thinking is at bottom the irreducibly parochial affair that relativists have urged it is; then I cannot see that there would be much consolation in the realist's belief in real moral states of affairs which, accordingly, some moral cultures – and it could as well be ours – are presumably doomed to miss.

For the moral anti-realist, there will be no defensible analogue of the scientific realist's thought that the real progress of science is measured by the extent to which our theories represent a reality whose nature owes nothing to our natures or the standards that inform our conception of responsible discourse about it. It will not be possible to regard the disciplined formation of a moral view as a seriously representational mode of function, or as a form of activity in which we respond to states of affairs which, precisely because they are at the service of the explanation of other things, can be put to serious work in explaining the course assumed by these responses. But my point has been that those concessions need not enforce the dilemma: either exile ethics from the realm of truth or dilute the concept of truth to the point of vacuity. So: what is so alarming about the prospect of moral anti-realism?

There may be a *psychological* problem: a tendency to cease to *identify* with those of one's opinions which philosophy discloses to lack an external sanction – to suffer a loss of moral problems, as it were. But I do not think that a clear-headed moral anti-realist ought for one moment to feel impelled to a general moral tolerance. Such a tolerance accepts that no differences of moral opinion need involve anything worthy of criticism. But while the anti-realist will have to accept that such differences need involve nothing worth regarding as *cognitive* shortcoming – as deficiency in representation, substantially conceived – the ordinary view will remain available that shortcoming may nevertheless often be involved, albeit an irreducibly *moral* shortcoming, a type of failing which can be appreciated only from a committed moral point of view.

In general – I guess the point is obvious enough – the immediate price of anti-realism about morals is merely that the gravity of moral judgement will lack an external sanction. When one is asked, 'Why bother to try to arrive at correct moral opinion?', the only available answer will be: because such an opinion informs *better* conduct – better, that is, from a moral point of view. The value of moral truth will thus be an instrumental, moral value. It is common to think that there are, by contrast, intrinsic, general values associated with pure discovery, understanding and knowledge of the real world. Properly to characterise and to understand such values seems to me to be a very difficult task. In any case, for the moral anti-realist, that kind of value cannot attach to moral truth. But I think it has seemed important that it should only because of the tendency of philosophers to suppose that there is nothing for truth to be that is not associated with value of that sort.

'What more could a sensible moral realist want?' What those whose intuitive inclination is to moral realism really want, I suggest, is not truth as representation – realism as properly understood – but a certain kind of objectivity in moral appraisal: ideally, precisely that a tendency towards convergence in the conception of what is morally important and how much importance it has, be indeed intrinsic to moral thinking itself. How much, and what kinds of moral appraisal may indeed contain the seeds of such convergence seems to me a great – perhaps the greatest – unresolved question in moral philosophy. My argument has been that the question has nothing to do with moral realism, but arises within the anti-realist camp.[13]

University of St. Andrews
St. Andrews KY16 9AL
Scotland

[13] Thanks to questioners at the Reading conference and at the presentation of this material as a public lecture at the University of Kansas in October 1994.

II

TRUTH IN ETHICS

Bernard Williams

I shall start with two thoughts which prima facie present a difficulty right from the beginning. The first is that truth in ethics is an important subject. The second is that, on a plausible view of the matter, truth in ethics is not a very important subject.

The reason for these two considerations coming together is this. Truth in ethics might seem an important subject because it bears very closely on certain questions such as objectivity, the possibility of ethical knowledge, and hence – and this I take to be a particularly significant question in this area – the nature of ethical authority, if there is such a thing: that is, why one person's views on ethical topics can be worth more than another's. So if truth in ethics is related to such questions, truth in ethics should be an important subject.

However, on a plausible view of the matter, truth in ethics is not in *itself* such an important question, because the question of truth in ethics is not itself any of those questions about objectivity, the possibility of ethical knowledge, and so forth.

I think that in this point I agree effectively with Crispin Wright. This may be (indeed I think it is) contrary to some things I wrote quite a long time ago, particularly perhaps in 'Consistency and Realism',[1] but I certainly don't wish to go back over those old writings. Now, at least, I should like to say, and here I am broadly agreeing with Wright,[2] that truth *in itself* isn't much. As I think Wright has shown, the conclusion that truth in itself isn't much follows from what I take to be an undeniable starting point, namely the soundness of Tarski's equivalence. If we can start from anything in the question of truth, we can start from the idea that '*p*' is true just in case that *p*.

Exactly how Tarski's equivalence is to be formulated, for instance with regard to relativisation to a language or otherwise, is a further question, and indeed it is a question to which I shall return later. What is not undeniable is any given philosophical interpretation of what Tarski's equivalence means. For instance,

[1] Reprinted in my *Problems of the Self* (Cambridge: Cambridge University Press, 1973).
[2] See his *Truth and Objectivity* (Cambridge, MA: Harvard University Press, 1992).

Popper held that Tarski's equivalence is the best expression of the correspondence theory of truth. Equally, it has been held that Tarski's equivalence is the best expression of the redundancy theory of truth, because it *displays* the idea that truth is a fundamentally disquotational notion.

But Tarski's equivalence does not express any such theory, and the fact that it's been taken by authoritative and competent commentators to express both the correspondence theory and the redundancy theory seems itself good evidence that it does not express any such theory. In particular, Tarski's equivalence does not express the redundancy theory. If you have Tarski's equivalence and no more, that is not equivalent to the following theory: truth is explained by Tarski's equivalence and no more.

However, we can learn something from the relations of Tarski's equivalence to the redundancy theory, in favour of what (again like Wright) I shall call *minimalism* with respect to truth. The mere fact that an account of truth has to accommodate Tarski's equivalence surely creates a strong presumption (for instance) that truth is not an epistemic concept.

It is certainly a necessary condition of qualifying for a truth predicate that ethical statements are statements: they are involved in speech acts of the assertive kind, they permit embedding and various other kinds of syntactic manipulation which are associated with the sorts of things that are statements, assertions, bearers of truth value. These syntactic phenomena, as we might call them, have to be honoured in any account of ethical statements. But how heavy a burden does the fact that these syntactic phenomena have to be honoured in any account of ethical statements impose on us? The answer depends on what our expectations are of semantic theory.

For instance, Hare made a definite semantic claim, namely that indicative and apparently assertoric moral statements were in fact universal imperatives.[3] Of course that claim involved an immediate semantic problem, of how such an analysis could be reconciled with the surface phenomena, and this gave rise to the machinery of phrastics, neustics, tropics, and so forth. A more recent example of someone who thinks that there is a heavy onus to discharge here is Alan Gibbard.[4] Gibbard wishes to reconcile an expressive view of ethical statements with the syntactic phenomena, and in order to

---

[3] See Hare, *Language of Morals* (Oxford: Clarendon Press, 1952).
[4] Gibbard, *Wise Choices, Apt Feelings* (Oxford: Clarendon Press, 1990).

do this, he has produced a semantic theory that is a fairly elaborate model-theoretic account of norms.

On the other hand, if you look at Simon Blackburn's 'quasi-realism',[5] you see a different picture: it represents, I think, a different expectation of semantic theory. As I understand Blackburn's view, he doesn't require any more work *at this point.* That is to say, he doesn't feel it necessary to do the kind of thing that Gibbard does in giving a model-theoretic or any similar semantics to reconcile the syntactic phenomena with an expressive view. The statements in question, on Blackburn's view, simply behave like statements. He supplements this with a metaphysical or epistemological account, which he thinks explains why the statements, illusorily in his view, bear an appearance of realism.

I'm not going to pursue that issue. It's not one on which I have any interesting view. I just draw attention to the fact that it's a disputed question how big a weight has to be picked up simply in virtue of reconciling some general metaethical view about the status of ethical beliefs with the surface syntactic phenomena that allow ethical statements to be statements.

I'm going to assume minimalism in the following form. There are two sets of what might be called *surface facts* with regard to ethical discourse. First, it is well regimented syntactically in the mode of indicative assertion (it allows embedding, conditionals, and all the sorts of things we are familiar with in that department). Second, utterances are assessed under the title of truth for their appropriateness, acceptability, or whatever. (My reference to 'appropriateness' and 'acceptability' here are not meant to beg any questions against truth.)

We may also accept the fact – less on the surface – that such assessments of ethical statements do not directly take the content of the ethical assertions to be determined by the speaker's psychological states. They are not taken to be truths in the mode of autobiographical subjectivism (except of course in very special cases where an ethical statement is of that character – some ethical statements, after all, are of an autobiographical character).

I take minimalism to say that the surface facts just mentioned do not by themselves determine the answer to substantive questions about realism, objectivism, cognitivism, or more generally the status of ethical statements, nor do they determine anything about

[5] Blackburn, *Spreading the Word* (Oxford: Clarendon Press, 1984); *Essays in Quasi-Realism* (New York: Oxford University Press, 1993).

the authority, if there is such a thing, of some ethical speakers as against others. To answer those questions, you have to go beyond the surface facts and not just note the practices of assertion, denial, appropriate syntactic regimentation and so on, but ask for the point of the practices of assertion, denial, argument, inquiry and so on, in the course of which these surface facts are displayed. The substantive questions in ethics about realism, objectivism, cognitivism, and so on, are questions not just about the existence of the surface facts, nor indeed about the adequacy of the surface facts to support the application of the word 'true'. The question is about the point in the ethical case of practices such as assertion, denial, and truth ascription.

At this point, we *do* encounter concepts of the cognitive kind. The point here is not that truth in ethics, any more than it is anywhere else, is itself a cognitive concept. It isn't. Rather the question of how much truth in ethics comes to, what it does for us, how much we should care about it, can only be discussed in terms of concepts such as knowledge. It is this emphasis that leads into questions about the cognitive.

You might say, and I think this is quite a helpful way of viewing the matter, that such questions about the status of ethics (questions about realism, objectivism, cognitivism and so on) concern not so much whether the discourse of ethics can support ascriptions of truth, but rather what the value of truth is for ethics. It's in the area of the value of truth that these issues come out.

This raises a point more general than one confined to ethics. If we consider the idea of the value of truth – and I'm not supposing that this is one homogeneous thing: there are quite a number of things that are the values of truth – a natural assumption is that what you have to do first is to determine what truth is for some region of discourse, and then you'll be in a position to ask about the value of truth in relation to that region of discourse. However, what I'd like to suggest is, roughly speaking, that we should proceed the other way round: what we should do is hold on to a minimalist account of truth everywhere and then the question of the value of truth in a given area will help us to see what more we should say about truth in that area.

When I refer to the value of truth, I don't mean the value of p's being true. Just in virtue of Tarski's equivalence, the value of p's being true is typically the value of p, if there is such a thing. For instance, contrary to the evidences and contrary to what everybody else says, this lady believes that her child survived the crash. She is in fact right. It's true her son survived the crash, and it is a good thing that her belief is true. But why it's a good thing that her belief is true is simply that it's a good thing that her son survived. This is not the value of truth, but the value of survival.

But there are other connections – and this is where the value of truth comes in – where the value of a belief's being true is not just a matter of the value of p where p expresses that belief. The value of truth in general is constituted by our relations to such truths for various such relations. It involves such things as the value of getting to know the truth, of continuing to look for the truth, of asserting the truth because it's true, of taking steps not to deceive oneself into thinking that p is false when it is in fact true, the value of identifying people whose information on the question whether p is likely to be true information, and so on. And it can involve such matters with which we're all familiar, for instance, in the law of libel, whether truth is a defence, whether, for instance, utterances that would otherwise be negatively valued should receive some positive value because those utterances were true. In all these connections, it seems to me, we can further our understanding of truth beyond the minimalist universal account of truth, by understanding the values of truth and, indeed, truthfulness.

The way in which the term 'truth' has turned up in all these formulations, formulations I associate with what I broadly call the value of truth, is unfavourable to the redundancy theory. The fact that we want to use 'truth' in such interlocking ways in talking about the value of truth illustrates one of the dimensions in which our concept of truth has to go beyond what is offered by the redundancy theory. Certainly the limited treatment that the value of truth has received from the redundancy theory has not been particularly auspicious.

Horwich's book, the best known recent exposition of the redundancy theory, provides an example.[6] In it, there is a brief passage about the value of truth. Horwich says that when one attaches a value to truth, what one wants is to believe p if and only if p.[7] He says 'if and only if', so it's not only that I wish all my beliefs to be true, but that I wish to believe all truths. The desire for accuracy is conflated with the desire for omniscience. This is a mistake, but it is not an unmotivated slip on Horwich's part. Horwich has grasped the point that in having an interest in the

---

[6] Paul Horwich, *Truth* (Oxford: Blackwell, 1990).
[7] Op. cit., p. 65.

truth I have an interest in acquiring some true beliefs and probably not trivial ones. That is, he doesn't wish to commit himself to what Popper often pointed out, correctly, to be a weakness of the attitude towards truth shown by (for instance) quite a lot of Oxford philosophers, namely that their only motivation was to avoid error: as Popper pointed out, an easy way to do that is not to have any beliefs at all. Horwich's formula, 'I attach a value to truth if I want to believe that p if and only if p', does pay dim homage to the idea that you want to have some true beliefs as well as wanting all your beliefs to be true. But his formula, clearly, is a crude shot at what the value of truth could be.

Horwich attaches to his formula an unnecessary further claim, that the value of truth should principally be identified with the pragmatic value of the consequences of having true beliefs. That doesn't follow at all. Why he might think it follows is clear: truth does so little work in redundancy theory that he's very suspicious of any notion of the value of truth which transcends the value of my behaving in a way appropriate to p when p, which is what he offers us.

Redundancy theory, as it has been developed so far, has not well handled the notion of the value of truth, and I think that the various motivations and interests we join under the heading of 'the value of truth' are such that minimalism will have to help itself to more than anything that is on offer from redundancy theory.

The value of truth in a given area, then, is a good focus for inquiry into how much further we should go beyond the surface facts which are the support of minimalism. The next point is, I think, important, but I shall have to leave it somewhat obscure because there is not time to develop it at adequate length. The fact that we are to investigate these questions in terms of the value of truth does not imply that we attach any particular value to truths *about value*. Truth is valuable to us, we seek truth, for various reasons, and it does not follow that we set any particular value on acquiring truth about value. People tend to say that, if it is important to have true beliefs, there can be nothing more important to have true beliefs about than questions of value. This simply assumes that the answers we need to questions about value must recommend themselves because they are truths; but whether this is so is one of the questions we want to investigate. What we must ask is how far the value that we attach to getting it right about values must itself take the form of the various things that we group under the value of truth. We must ask how far the authority of knowledge, for instance, the value of honest inquiry, and other values of truthfulness, all of which are very firmly rooted when we are dealing with non-value matters, carry over into inquiries (if that's what we can call them) into value.

It's worth for instance remembering here that when people have invoked the values of truth and truthfulness in political matters, their natural paradigm is not that of preserving truth about some moral matter: they want to preserve the capacity to think truthfully about other matters. When Orwell said in *1984*, 'Freedom is the freedom to say that twice two is four', he was picking on precisely this point: it is manifest truth of various kinds, the resistance to lies, that the political order has to protect.

Another way one can put it is this: one of the things in valuing truth we have to protect ourselves against is wishful thinking, which along with self-deception is a particularly insidious enemy of truthfulness. Now, we might ask whether there is such a thing as wishful thinking about what is right. Or is it rather that we can get to wrong conclusions about what is right because we go in for wishful thinking about other things? The point I'm making is that we ought to ask how straightforwardly the values of truth with regard to self-deception, wishful thinking, and so on, carry over into the field of value.

I am not going to say anything more about this today, because at this point I'm going to remove a fiction which I have so far sustained and which it is important to remove. This fiction, which constantly affects discussions of this subject, is that there is a homogeneous class of ethical assertions, and that, in considering the advance beyond the minimalist account, we need to say the same things about all of them. The surface facts are in common between all these statements, of course, because the surface facts are facts about them just as statements. But once we go beyond this we find that they have important differences, and these differences are important in relation to the issues about realism, cognitivism, and so on.

I have claimed elsewhere that an important distinction here is that between statements deploying what I call *thin* ethical concepts and statements deploying what I call *thick* ethical concepts. Thin ethical concepts are concepts like 'good', 'right', and 'wrong'. 'Abortion is wrong', if anybody makes so unqualified a claim, is an ethical statement that deploys a thin, in fact the thinnest, ethical concept. Contrast with this ethical statements deploying concepts such as 'cruel', 'brutal', 'dishonest', 'treacherous', or which describe people as chaste, kind-hearted, or whatever. Such statements, in my terms, deploy thick ethical concepts.

Quite a lot can be said about the distinction itself and how exactly it works, but, although I'm going to be saying more about thick concepts, I won't elaborate on the distinction further. Obviously, in some sense, thick concepts have a higher empirical content. It's worth adding, as Samuel Scheffler has pointed out,[8] that there is an important class of concepts that lie between the thick and the thin, notably the concept of justice. There is more to it than to a concept like 'right': that an action is just is *one reason* it can be right. On the other hand, the content of 'just' is in a certain way indeterminate or disputable or open to a variety of conceptions.

I take it that assertions can be minimally true whether they deploy thin or thick concepts. The surface facts apply to all such assertions.

There is a range of pressures that move some philosophers to focus on thin concepts. Some think that thin concepts represent (you might say) the moral essence. These are people whom Susan Hurley has called 'centralists', people who think that a thick ethical concept is constructed around a central core of the thin, and that the ethical force of the thick really lies in the thin.[9] There are other motivations more complexly related to the primacy of the thin: there is a certain fundamentally Kantian project in which the aim is to build ethical philosophy on thin ethical concepts, and I shall say something about this at the end. There are other writers who concentrate on the thin for the opposite reason, that they are hostile to the status of ethical discourse. They see the thin as the crucially weak spot, because it is about thin statements that people most spectacularly and manifestly disagree.

Other philosophers want to start with the thick. Some do this because they think it's a peculiarly strong spot. I want to start with the thick. Certainly for the subject under discussion here it's the right place to start, and, in a sense, I do think that it's a peculiarly strong spot, but, as I shall explain, I don't think it's as strong as some of the neo-Aristotelian writers who favour this theme think it is. But I think that the reason for this is more interesting than those typically brought forward by subjectivist or expressivist critics.

When we think about thick concepts, statements containing such

---

[8] Scheffler, 'Morality Through Thick and Thin', *Philosophical Review* 96 (1987), p. 417.

[9] Hurley, 'Objectivity and Disagreement', in Ted Honderich (ed.), *Morality and Objectivity* (London: Routledge and Kegan Paul, 1985).

concepts manifestly satisfy the minimalist conditions (they fall in very easily with the surface facts) – but seemingly they display *more*. They seem to display the opportunity for a larger set of the notions associated with truth and indeed the value of truth. For instance, they involve the application of the concept of knowledge. They invite us to think that, with regard to statements involving these concepts, it might be pointful and helpful to say that some people as opposed to others might *know*. That's so, I think, if we think of a plausible construction of the point of the concept of knowledge. If we have a construction on the lines of that offered in Edward Craig's admirable *Knowledge and the State of Nature*,[10] one in which the point of the concept of knowledge is that of helping us to identify reliable informants, then when we ask the question 'Is there such a thing as ethical knowledge?' we've got a point to the question – the point: is there such a thing, in ethics, as a helpful informant? If we concentrate on thick concepts, we do indeed have something like the notion of a helpful informant. We have the notion of a helpful advisor. This is somebody who may be better at seeing that a certain outcome, policy, or way of dealing with the situation falls under a concept of this kind, than we are in our unassisted state, and better than other people who are less good at thinking about such matters.

This does seem to be a way in which the concept of knowledge can be brought into ethics that doesn't run into the difficulties encountered by other ways of bringing in that concept. For instance, it looks a lot better than a model of ethical knowledge as theoretical. We've all been brought up to know that in a sense there are no moral experts, yet people are in a way trying to recreate the notion of a moral expert in relation to applied ethics. There are areas in which having a degree in (e.g.) medical ethics is thought to qualify someone for making a certain class of judgements. The idea of such an expertise is implausible – not many people are going to say 'Well, I didn't understand the professor's argument for his conclusion that abortion is wrong, but since he is qualified in the subject, abortion probably is wrong.' But even if we think there is something wrong about the theoretical model of moral expertise, we do have an idea of a helpful advisor, who can see that something falls under a certain thick concept; he or she can see, for instance, the situation as being an example of treachery, something that hadn't occurred to the rest of us. In this, there seems to be a handle

---

[10] Oxford: Clarendon Press, 1990.

for the application of the concept of knowledge. If that's right, then we have a bit more than the minimalism associated with the surface facts. For here we have a value attached to the notion of finding the truth that ties in with, is of a piece with, the general point (under a plausible construction) of the concept of knowledge.

It's worth saying also that, although this is a useful way of looking at a certain class of advisors, it isn't in my view correct to suppose that a helpful and constructive advocate of a moral outlook has to be construed as someone who knows that outlook to be true. I think there are ways in which someone can be a helpful and constructive advocate of a moral outlook without that being the centre of the argument at all. For instance, he may be able to show you by his discourse that that moral outlook will help you, will make your life more of a life, will set you free, and this can be true of other projects which are not assessed primarily in the dimension of the true. The point will be, not that the moral outlook is true, but that the moral outlook can give you a life worth living (though you may think 'a life worth living' is itself an ethical concept that involves the notion of the truth).

Let us grant that under thick concepts we can extend the set of interests associated with the value of truth beyond the territory of minimalism and the surface facts. Let us grant that this is a dimension in which the concept of knowledge can begin to do some work. We then face the point that not everyone shares the same thick concepts. The vocabulary of thick concepts is not homogeneous in a pluralistic society, nor homogeneous over time or between different societies.

This is well illustrated if we think about a formula David Wiggins has introduced, 'there is nothing else to think but that p'.[11] Wiggins has introduced us to a situation in which I wonder what to think, you then explain that for this and this and this reason things stand in a certain way, and I conclude that there is nothing else to think but that p. In Wiggins's argument, this is associated with the notion of a vindicatory explanation, which for him is tied up with a very broadly Peircean notion of truth. I leave that aside and concentrate on the formula 'there is nothing else to think but that p'. Wiggins thinks this formula can be applied equally to ethical and non-ethical propositions. Just as there can be nothing else to think but that the sum of these numbers is 3,456, or that this tyre

---

[11] 'Moral Cognitivism, Moral Relativism and Motivating Moral Beliefs', *Proceedings of the Aristotelian Society* 91 (1990–91).

has a hole in it, so there may be nothing else to think but that this action is cruel.

Wiggins's formula is implicitly relativised in various ways. Obviously it's relativised to someone in a certain evidential situation. There is a less obvious relativisation as well. For clearly in all these cases it won't literally be true that there is nothing else to think about the given situation or circumstance but that p. There is always more than one true thing to think about any situation. What 'there is nothing else to think but that p' must mean is: there is nothing else to think, *given the question whether p*. This implicitly relativises the claim to those who use the concepts involved in the question whether p, and this is extremely important.

Consider the case of the boys who torture the cat. The boys do a wanton and hideous thing to the cat, which causes the cat great pain. Wiggins says there is nothing else to think but that it was a cruel thing to do. Unfortunately, however, there is something else to think but that it was a cruel thing to do – for instance that it was fun, which is what the boys thought. True, if you use the concept 'cruel', there is nothing else to think but that their behaviour was cruel. But there is nothing in the situation, or in the discourse of these other people, that can recruit somebody into using the concept 'cruel' if they don't already, unless of course on this occasion they learn that concept. They might be so shocked or upset by the situation that they acquire the concept.

This draws our attention to an extremely important form of ethical difference – namely that between those who do and those who don't use a certain concept. There was a marvellous moment in one of Oscar Wilde's trials when counsel read to Wilde a passage from one of his works and asked 'Mr. Wilde, don't you think that's obscene?' Wilde replied ' "Obscene" is not a word of mine.' This illustrates that the question of what your repertoire of thick concepts is reveals your own or your society's ethical attitude. An important difference between different ethical cultures concerns what thick ethical concepts do any work in them. There can also be a diachronic difference here. An example is the concept of chastity. This concept used to do a lot of work in relation to sexual ethics. (I take it the concept of chastity is one that has some depth – that is, it doesn't simply mean 'celibate' but rather ties together a range of ideas about sexual purity.)

This phenomenon underlies a claim which I made in *Ethics and the Limits of Philosophy* in terms that some people have found confusing or unnecessarily provocative – namely the claim that reflection in ethics can destroy knowledge. I would in any case like to say that all I claimed was that reflection can destroy knowledge, not that it must do so, but it has been disputed whether it even can destroy knowledge. If the situation is simply that what people used to believe to be true, they now believe to be false, they wouldn't think of what they earlier believed as being, at that earlier time, knowledge. Nor did I mean something unintelligible, namely that the very thing that used to be true has now become false. What I had in mind was the situation in which they no longer have the concept with which they used to express a certain class of beliefs. They lose a concept, and so cease to have a disposition that expresses itself in categorising the world in those terms.

It's also important that they don't have to say that they've made a discovery, e.g., that there is no such virtue as chastity. If they discovered this, they'd have to regard their earlier remarks, or the remarks of their ancestors in this regard, as presumably either false or in some way failing through presuppositional failure. It would be like discovering there was no such thing as phlogiston. They *might* say that there was no such virtue as chastity, but the point I want to emphasise is that this isn't forced on them. Least of all is it forced on them by the surface facts, or indeed even by a rather wider range of semantic facts.

I don't think there is a grave problem in formulating this problem, if anyone wants to, in terms that fit into an elementary theory of truth. Statements of the kind 'X is chaste' and 'X is not chaste' are true, when they're true, in some language L, which is a certain ethical language but not the same as *our* ethical language L_o because the languages differ at least in the respect that one contains the concept of chastity and the other one doesn't. This doesn't mean that when some speaker of L gives approval to an utterance of another speaker of L, he or she is awarding that speaker only the qualified approval 'what you said was true *in L*'. As David Lewis has pointed out, if a person's utterance is true in L, and the person is speaking L, then the person's utterance is true. To use an illustration introduced by Philip Percival in a recent article,[12] Borg's performance on what we call the tennis court made him the victor at tennis. Of course there is another possible game, quennis, at which he was the loser (roughly, you lose at quennis just in case you win at tennis.) But the fact is that Borg was playing tennis, so he was indeed the winner, since that was the game he was playing.

---

[12] Percival, 'Absolute Truth', *Proceedings of the Aristotelian Society* 94 (1994), p. 191.

It's not that his winning is something qualified – that he is a 'winner at tennis'. Indeed, what defines his winning is the concept of winning at tennis, just as what governs these people's utterances is truthfulness in L; but they get the marks for saying true things precisely because they're speaking L.

Someone can come to understand this ethical language L without its being that person's own language. That's the ethnographic stance. A person who is exposed to the society can, for instance, impersonate an L-speaker. The visitor to the society is, let us say, an L_o-speaker. He impersonates L-speakers, and may temporarily become indistinguishable from an L-speaker even to himself. There are whole days perhaps in which his world is the world of the L-speaker. In this case, he will in speaking follow the rule of truthfulness-in-L. Reverting to his role as external commentator, he may remark that the utterances of a given L-speaker are true. He will be following the rule of truthfulness-in-L.

What he can't do is to generate a Tarski-equivalent right hand side in his own language L_o for the claim that (e.g.) 'X is chaste' is true in L. The reason he can't do this is that, given the way in which we set up the case, the expressive powers of his own language are different from those of the native language precisely in the respect that the native language contains an ethical concept which his doesn't. If we suppose his ethical language is based largely on thin ethical concepts, you might say the expressive powers of his language are weaker. Of course someone identified with his language would say that, even if it is expressively weaker, it is ethically stronger because it lacks all this apparatus of ethical concepts that the natives' language contains.

Granted the fact, which I find undeniable, that different societies' thick concepts are not simply homogeneous, don't simply map on to each other, we have a perfectly coherent account of what truthfulness in L is and what its relation can be to the language of an observer.

I've suggested that thick concepts provide the most promising area in ethics for delivering more than minimal truth, more than simply the surface facts. They provide examples of ethical statements that can not only be true but also be pointfully be said to be known by people. But of course these facts don't remove all disagreement. This is not simply because some or all of the parties are ignorant, but because of a lack of conceptual homogeneity. The practical judgements that follow from the use of ethical concepts in one such ethical language or culture are not the same as those that

follow from the use of other thick ethical concepts, or again from
the use of thin concepts in other ethical languages. As the
ethnographic stance illustrates, this doesn't mean these languages
are mutually unintelligible. You can learn the other language
by the well-known method of pretending to be a speaker of it, by
identifying historically, ethnographically, or simply sympathetic-
ally with a speaker of it. It still doesn't become, by that fact, your
language.

Since the application of thick ethical concepts typically gives
reasons for courses of action, we get, as a result, univocal
disagreements at the level of practical reason that can be expressed
in thin concepts. For we get to a matter of practical decision where
we get some term like 'right' and 'wrong', and one group thinks a
certain course of action is right and another group thinks it wrong.
Those thin concepts I take to be, at the end of the line, univocal.
That is a focused disagreement. A focused disagreement doesn't
represent all the bases of the disagreement, which lie in two
different ethical languages or different ethical structures of the
world, but it certainly is a disagreement.

I should say in passing that, although I am sure there has to be a
univocal sense of 'right' and 'wrong' closely related to practical
reason such that these two parties can come to understand that
what one thinks is right the other thinks is wrong, I'm not in the
least clear that this is identical with the terms 'right' and 'wrong'
that turn up so often in ethics. I don't know what these terms, in
the ways they are so often used in ethics, mean (I'm not sure that
those who use these terms in ethics know what they mean either.)
But at some level very near to practical decision there has to be a
term that is used univocally in different cultures.

We know that when people say that they want real truth in
ethics, above all when they say that they want objectivity in ethics,
they want more than the local language of thick concepts and the
associated minimal truth. Perhaps we are now in a position to see
what it is they want. They want there to be one canonical,
homogeneous ethical language. They want it to be conceptually
homogeneous across cultures, and across disagreements within our
culture (across pluralism).

At this point we encounter two strategies. The Kantians and
Utilitarians take the piece of the ethical language that is seemingly,
and hoped to be, univocal – the thin bit – and try to get it to do all
the ethical conceptual work. This gives us conceptual homogeneity
(at least it does if we get it working better than the use of 'right' and

'wrong' actually works). The trouble is that it leaves us with all the disagreements, and the endlessly unhelpful debates about which theory or decision procedure or constructive undertaking can, as it were, be wished on the other party in a way that will give us not only conceptually univocal and homogeneous conclusions but also a substantively identical decision procedure. Under certain assumptions where it is very near to a political order, and the constraints on the political order are quite high, and so on, one can get a little way in that direction. But experience tends to show that it's not going to get all the way in generating precisely the kind of outlook that can be saluted as objective and agreed.

The other strategy is to behave as the neo-Aristotelians do. They rightly concentrate on the thick part, which offers a high order of such things as convergence and knowledge, and so promises substantive additions to mere minimalism. The trouble is that the thick part isn't conceptually homogeneous. Not everybody shares the same such language.

There are, again, two different ways of proceeding from this point. You can simply ignore the fact that not everybody shares the same thick ethical concepts. This is the method adopted by those who go on as though it were Aristotle's, or possibly St. Thomas's, time: the move from an older world to late twentieth-century Los Angeles is made in one large jump, which is sociologically optimistic, to say the least of it. I don't think this way is very helpful. These neo-Aristotelians are rather too Aristotelian.

The other way is to assume that there must be an underlying theory of the virtues such that cultural variation, while acknowledged, can be understood as a surface adaptation. On this view, there is a kind of deep structure to thick ethical concepts, and we can understand local variants as appropriate relativisations to circumstances (e.g., in certain social circumstances thinking in terms of chastity really is appropriate). Alternatively, we may be given a deep structure account together with a theory of error, so it will be said, e.g., that chastity never was a good concept for thinking about sexual behaviour, because it was always a patriarchally imposed device. In such a case, you have the promise of a theory of error which is non-trivial, if difficult to honour.

Given the aim to go beyond minimal truth and the surface facts and uncover one canonical, homogeneous set of thick ethical concepts, one has to accept (what some neo-Aristotelian theorists ignore) the facts of historical and social variation, which are simply undeniable. The project then becomes that of understanding those variations in terms of a deep structure of thick concepts together with appropriate social relativisations and, possibly, a theory of error. I think the most optimistic thing to be said about this project is that we simply don't know whether it can succeed. Perhaps it's possible that some such structure might emerge. But I still doubt it. I also doubt to what extent it would be other than an ethical project. The ethical dimension of such assessment – of such a trans-historical, trans-social, interpretation – will be so high that I do not know whether it could actually gain ground that might be acknowledged by all parties as being a step beyond minimalist truth into objectivism.

There are two points to be emphasised, whatever one's thoughts or hopes about this project are.

The first is that no such theory now exists. To pretend that it does is simply bluff. When writers remark 'there is really only one set of virtues that contribute to human flourishing, and they are differently interpreted under different societal arrangements', they are drawing on an account which we don't know to contain any funds at all.

The second point is that the answers to these questions are not entailed by conclusions in the theory of truth for ethical statements. We've got minimal truth and we have the surface facts and we can respect the surface facts and under favourable circumstances we can have more than that. We can have convergence, and we can have (I suggest) some knowledge. Some issues of objectivity which seek to go beyond this lead to questions of what ethical concepts we should have, and how we should answer questions of what ethical concepts we should have. But that issue is not going to be resolved by further investigations of ethical truth as such. It's not a semantic issue we're concerned with here. It's a blend of an ethical issue on the one hand and an anthropological or hermeneutical issue on the other.

Corpus Christi College
University of Oxford
Oxford OX1 4JF
England

OBJECTIVE AND SUBJECTIVE IN ETHICS, WITH TWO POSTSCRIPTS ABOUT TRUTH

David Wiggins

I

Objective/nonobjective: The suggestion I defend is this. A subject matter is objective (or relates to an objective reality) if and only if there are questions about it (and enough questions about it) that admit of answers that are substantially true – simply and plainly true, that is.

What is plain truth? What is truth like? Elsewhere (see also the two postscripts), I have tried to show how one might enumerate the marks of the concept of truth, and on what basis. ('Marks' in Frege's sense: see 'Concept and Object'.) Here, and for present purposes, perhaps it will be enough to illustrate how, contrary to what might be expected, it is conceivable that moral beliefs or judgements should possess one of the most, meta-ethically speaking, troublesome marks of truth. The mark might be given like this: If it is true that p, then, in so far as it can be known that p, someone can believe that p precisely because p. The argument for this requirement upon truth can be derived from the exigencies of interpretation, or it can be derived from our intuitive idea that for a subject matter to be aimed at truth is for it to be aimed to furnish those who involve themselves in it with grounds for various beliefs which are grounds for the truth of those beliefs.

Let it be clear that to show that it is not excluded that moral judgements should have the mark of truth we are concerned with here is not yet to show that they can have all the other marks that truth would require. The most that it can demonstrate is how moral judgements might indeed possess one potentially troublesome mark, if things look not too bleak in respect of the others.

'To believe that p precisely because p'. This is only a slogan, to be understood in the light of diverse examples, in which we seek to show a common pattern. The common pattern is something like this: one comes to believe that p precisely because p only if the best full explanation of one's coming to believe that p requires the giver of the explanation to adduce in his explanation either the very fact that p or something which leaves no room to deny that p. This is to say that his explanation conforms to one of the following forms. 'Look, the cat is on the mat. So, given John's perceptual capacities and his presence near that cat, no wonder he believes the cat is on the mat.' (This explanation answers the question: 'why does John believe the cat is on the mat?') Or again (in reply to the question 'why does Peter believe $7 + 5 = 12$?'), consider an explanation that runs on this pattern. Look, $7 + 5 = 12$; the calculating rule leaves room for no other answer. [Explainer shows this.] So no wonder Peter, who understands the calculating rule, believes that $7 + 5 = 12$. (Why refer here to subject *and* interpreter? To stress the complementarity of 1st/3rd person aspects of certainty, conviction and knowledge.)

Let us call such an explanation for the existence of a belief a *vindicatory explanation* of that belief. Let Ethical Objectivism then be or, better, imply the thesis that the subject matter of morality admits vindicatory explanations of (at least some) moral beliefs. An example might run as follows: Look, slavery is wrong, it's wrong because . . . [here are given many, many considerations, fully spelled out, appealing to what someone already knows if he knows what 'wrong' means, and working together to leave nothing else to think but that slavery is wrong]; so no wonder twentieth century Europeans, who would accept that . . . and whose beliefs are so many of them downwind of such considerations as . . ., believe that slavery is wrong. They believe that it is wrong for just the reasons why it is wrong.

Ethical Objectivism, so characterised, represents a strongly but not crudely cognitivist conception of the subject matter of morals. It ought to be obvious that it is far from obvious whether the position is correct. We do not know for sure whether or how often we can put together considerations '. . .' that will combine to leave nothing else to think.

The opposite of 'objective' is 'non-objective'. It remains to be determined what the relation is of non-objective to subjective.

II

Subjective/non-subjective: My suggestion is this. A subject matter is subjective if it pertains to/arises from the states, responses (etc.) of conscious subjects and if questions about this subject matter are answerable to a standard that is founded in these states, responses (etc.) of subjects: or (where there is no question of identifying a standard at all) if questions about this subject matter are answerable only to these states, responses etc.

Because this is a wide and inclusive definition of 'subjective', ethical subjectivism can take various forms and receive various expressions:

– *Protagoras* [restricted]: man is the measure of all [valuational] things.
– [possible] *Hume*: x is good if and only if x is such as to arouse approbation.
– [real] *David Hume*: 'There is just so much vice or virtue in any character as every one places in it and 'tis impossible in this particular we can ever be mistaken.'[1] (The subjectivist can say something more subtle than this. Hume makes a start upon that in 'Of the Standard of Taste'.[2])
– *Refined Humean subjectivism*: x is good if and only if x is such as to *deserve* (NB) or *merit* approbation.[3]
– *Thomas Hobbes*: 'But whatsoever is the object of any mans Appetite or Desire; that is it, which he for his part calleth *Good*: And the object of his Hate, and Aversion, *Evill*; And of his Contempt, *Vile* and *Inconsiderable*. For these words of Good, Evill, and Contemptible, are ever used with relation to the person that useth them: There being nothing simply and absolutely so; nor any common Rule of Good and Evill, to be taken from the nature of the objects themselves; but from the Person of the man (where there is no Common-wealth;) or, (in a Common-wealth,) from the Person that representeth it; or from Arbitrator or Judge, whom men disagreeing shall by consent set up, and make his sentence the Rule thereof.'[4]
– [*All subjectivists*]: Ultimately statements of value are answerable only to such standards as are set by human feelings/responses. (NB: Contrary to what might be supposed, this does *not* restrict value to that which engages with human interests or promotes human advantage. It is up to the sentiments what they will engage with, or up to the sentiments together with the reasons that they give themselves for the stance they take up.)

[1] *Treatise of Human Nature* (1739–40), book 3 part 2 § 8. (In the second edition of Selby-Bigge and Nidditch's edition (Oxford: Clarendon Press, 1978), p. 547.)
[2] *Essays Moral, Political and Literary* (1741–42). Republished by Oxford University Press, 1963.
[3] Cf. A. J. Ayer, *Freedom and Morality* (Oxford: Clarendon Press, 1984) p. 30; and J. McDowell, 'Value and Secondary Qualities', in T. Honderich (ed.), *Morality and Objectivity: A Tribute to J. L. Mackie* (London: Routledge, 1985), pp. 117–20.
[4] *Leviathan*, (1651), book 1 chapter 6 (reprinted in Everyman's Library 1914, 1963, p. 24).

– *Vulgar subjectivism*: (a) '*x* is good', as said by me, means 'I like it' or (at best) (b) 'we like it'.

Some of these positions are more familiar than others. The objections to vulgar subjectivism are familiar. Variant (a) makes disagreement impossible. (See G. E. Moore, who seems unaware of subjectivisms that are not exposed to this objection.[5]) Variant (b) misrepresents the content of disagreement. Against refined subjectivism, some may object that it depends on not analysing away the moral terms 'deserve'/'merit'. It is crucially important here whether the subjectivist does or does not take himself to need to engage in analysing away. It is doubtful that Hume, for instance, believing taste and morals to be 'altogether new creations', as he does, ought to believe that, in order to be for its existence or nature to be explained, moral language has to be analysed away.

If Hume is a subjectivist according to these proposals, then in what should he have said the subjectiveness of moral thought and language consisted? Perhaps in this: Value terms have their sense by being annexed to properties in objects that call for certain shareable responses – the responses to these objects that they *make appropriate*.[6]

III

Historical note. The *Oxford English Dictionary* under 'objective' says this. The scholastic philosophy made the distinction between what belongs to things *subjectivē* [Latin adverb] or as they are 'in themselves' (on the one hand) and (on the other) what belongs to them *objectivē* [Latin adverb] or as they are presented to consciousness. In later times the custom of considering the perceiving or thinking consciousness as pre-eminently 'the subject' brought about the different use of these words which now prevails in philosophy [and which prevails in our proposals]. According to this, what is considered as belonging to the perceiving or thinking self is called 'subjective' and what is considered as independent of the perceiving or thinking self is called in contrast 'objective'.

So 'objective' and 'subjective', as it were, changed places!

NB: in the last sentence of our report of *The Oxford English Dictionary*, the word 'objective' serves as an opposite of 'subjective'.

[5] G. E. Moore, *Ethics* (Oxford: Oxford University Press, 1912).
[6] Cf. McDowell, 'Values and Secondary Qualities'; and my 'Truth Invention and the Meaning of Life', *Proceedings of the British Academy* 62 (1976) reprinted in my *Needs, Values, Truth* (Oxford: Blackwell, 1987) and 'A Sensible Subjectivism', *ibid*.

We should have to explain this use by thinking of it as connoting what might less confusingly be called the *non-subjective*. The *general* explanation of the objective is better given as in § I above (or so I hold).

IV

Clearly the 'objective'/'non-objective' contrast and the 'non-subjective'/'subjective' contrast are two *different*, albeit connected, contrasts. When people contrast 'objective' and 'subjective', first ascertain that they're not scholastics. *Then* ascertain whether they have begun with the subjective and defined the objective by forming its complement: or whether they have begun with the objective and called its complement the 'subjective'. Ask also how they defined the one they began with. If they haven't done either of these things, then ask if they have done the best thing (which is what we have done here) and defined 'objective' and 'subjective' separately? If so, how? Bear in mind the awful possibility that they may not know what they're doing or what has been done on their behalf. In which case it will be an accident if they end up saying anything useful or intelligible.

It would be a long business, but not impossible, to pause here to describe in these terms the use that various philosophers have made of 'objective' and 'subjective' and the preconceptions they have attached (with or without justification) to the subjective, notably that of non-objectivity. We shall only pause long enough at this point to treat the case of Hume (who uses neither word). Hume has impressive arguments for the claim that moral judgements are subjective in the sense explicated here. In the *Treatise* he manifestly supposes that they are also not objective. (Contrast, however, p. 547 loc. cit. with p. 620 in Selby-Bigge and Nidditch.) This anti-objectivism is progressively qualified and relaxed in his subsequent writings, which are replete with optimism about the resources of moral argument and the prospects of principled agreement. He does not, however, avow anything tantamount to proper objectivism. It would have been open to him to do so, had he thought such a position true.

V

If you are satisfied so far, then pause, consolidate, and consider the following situation. Somebody says this to you: Never mind this terminological fuss. You don't need to. It's *obvious* how to distinguish the objective and the subjective. A paradigmatic instance of the objective would be the question of the outdoor temperature at Kew Gardens on May 20th, 1993 at noon G.M.T. A representative instance of the subjective would be the question of the fairness or otherwise of the scales operative on that day for the remuneration of the grades of gardener employed there on that day. Surely there is a manifest and conceptually overwhelming difference between these kinds of question.

The right reply to this is not to suggest that questions of the second sort might shade off into question of the first sort. Until the first thing is clearer, namely the point of the contrast being illustrated, that is simply feeble. (Shade off along what dimension of similarity?) The right reply is to ask what it is that the first instance is meant to be paradigmatic of and what the second instance is meant to be representative of. Until we know that, examples can scarcely clarify the distinction that purports to be introduced here. Is the objector's distinction of objective and subjective intended to sort things into two mutually exclusive kinds? (In which case more needs to be said about whether there are degrees of objectivity and more needs to be said about why the second example cannot aspire to any degree of objectivity.) Or is it a distinction that sorts into two only presumptively non-overlapping kinds? (In which case more needs to be said to argue the non-overlap of their extensions.) Or is it a distinction like that between being an animal and being a mouse, where the things distinguished are indeed distinct but being a mouse is simply a special case of being an animal? (There are other possibilities again.)

Similar tricks will be tried upon you concerning *fact* and *value*, or is and *ought* (or in the philosophy of mind with regard to the mental and physical). Such pairs can be introduced as definitionally exclusive, in which case they should be announced first as the fact/non-fact distinction and the *is*/non-*is* distinction, leaving the status of value and of *ought* to be argued on their merits. (Are valuational questions not factual questions? Why not? Are *ought* questions not a species of *is* questions?) Or these four terms can be introduced as distinct items, each being positively characterised. In which case, as we have seen, the question of their interrelation will remain open until it is argued further. Such still (after 2500 years) is the chaos in moral philosophy (and mental philosophy). Philosophers can confuse you in this matter without even intending to fool you or take advantage of you.

VI

So – if we define 'objective' positively as here (in terms of there being nothing else to think) and we define 'subjective' positively as here (in terms of answerability to a standard founded in sentiment), i.e. if that is how we decide to do things here – then it will be an open question whether some moral question might be both subjective *and* objective. Consider now the prospect of vindicating the consensus that slavery is wrong or unjust by considerations (not necessarily deductive) that both appeal to standards that are founded in sentiment and yet leave *nothing else to think* but that slavery is wrong. Taking a leaf from C. S. Peirce's book (cf. *Collected Papers*, V, 265), let me urge that what Peirce said of thinking in general might be said of discursive moral argument, namely that it is 'not to be conceived to "form a chain which is no stronger than its weakest link" ', but is to be conceived as 'a cable whose fibers may be ever so slender provided they are sufficiently numerous and intimately connected'. Ethical objectivism enters a very strong claim. It represents a form of high optimism about the latent resources of moral argument. But Peirce's model suggests a saner conception than others of what it would be to justify that optimism. Conclusive arguments can be made by gradual accumulation of the right sorts of consideration.

VII

The purpose of this lecture is not to champion Ethical Objectivism. It is to suggest what it turns on whether Ethical Objectivism is defensible. If the issue does turn on what it is claimed here to turn upon, then one of the chief issues in metaethics turns on the question of the actual and potential variety and strength of moral argument. This question cannot be answered without first engaging in moral argument or suasion and bringing to bear upon it the full variety of our moral ideas and the full range of our dialectical resources (deduction, analogy, abduction, etc.). There is no other way to test the strength and resilience of these ideas.

Two Postscripts

Unluckily, I was unable to give this lecture at the Reading Conference. Through the good offices of the Editor (to whom I am multiply indebted) and as part of his plan to show contributors

other contributors' efforts before publication, I have seen the
contributions of Crispin Wright and Bernard Williams – even as
they have seen mine. In so far as they refer to me, however
glancingly, I now respond.

Postscript I

Bernard Williams refers here and elswhere to the following
difficulty in the claim that there exists what I call a vindicatory
explanation for beliefs like the belief that slavery is wrong. He says
it is not enough to show that, when one describes the institution
of slavery as 'slavery' and one adduces ideas like 'injustice',
'inhumanity', 'exploitation', there is nothing else to think but that
slavery is wrong. It is not enough, because to show only this much
cannot suffice to show that there isn't any other way to categorize
institutions like (those we call) slavery. In which case there may be
other ways to evaluate such institutions.

In the paper of mine where the idea of a vindicatory explanation
is chiefly elaborated, I tried to anticipate the point that he is
making here.[7] In this paper there were two chief purposes. The first
was to formulate ethical cognitivism, or Ethical Objectivism, as I
call it here, in a fashion that would suit cognitivists and non-
cognitivists equally – i.e., in a fashion that foreclosed upon no
party. The second purpose was to make a start upon the question
whether the formulated position was correct. I therefore interpret
Williams's doubt as a doubt about the second purpose and as a
doubt about the very possibility of Ethical Objectivism succeeding.
So I read it as resting upon his *acceptance* of the formulation itself. I
hope that is not too optimistic.

Suppose that some person, Clarkson or Wilberforce, say, believes
that slavery is wrong, and suppose that someone else undertakes to
explain why it is that Clarkson or Wilberforce believes this.

It is common ground that the explainer does not have to show
that there was nothing else for the subject to have attended to. In
that epoch, Clarkson or Wilberforce could have attended equally
usefully to the question of the chemical composition of air, for
instance, or the question of the efficacy of proposed improvements
in the system of rotation of crops. It is not constitutive of our idea of
a fact or of a truth which is there to be grasped that it should
predominate over all other matters of interest or concern.

[7] See 'Moral Cognitivism, Moral Relativism and Motivating Moral Beliefs', *Proceedings of
the Aristotelian Society* 91 (1990–91), especially §§ 5, 6, 8, 12, this last section being the one
where Williams's doubt is anticipated.

Nor yet does the explainer of their beliefs have to show that there was no other point of view for Clarkson or Wilberforce to have taken up than that to which questions present themselves of right and wrong or just and unjust. What the explainer has to show is only this: why, *given* that these subjects, to whom the question of right or wrong posed itself, attended to the institution that we call 'slavery', (a) they grasped or categorized it as slavery and (b) they saw it as brutal, inhuman, exploitative, unjust and wrong.

The claim of Ethical Objectivism might then be that the best explanation of this attitude of Clarkson's or Wilberforce's coming into being exemplifies the following form. For moral purposes, there is no other way to categorize slavery than as slavery and, given that . . ., [here come the considerations en masse, given at any length necessary], there is nothing else to think, in the world as it is or was, but that slavery is brutal, inhuman, exploitative, unjust and wrong: so no wonder that Clarkson and Wilberforce, perceiving it in the world as it was, and aware that . . ., grasped or categorized the institution as slavery and saw it as brutal, inhuman, exploitative, unjust and wrong.

Let it be perfectly clear between Williams and me that Ethical Objectivism enters a very strong claim here. Let it also be clear that the claim that there is nothing else to think is absolute. It does not mean that there is nothing else *for us* to think. That has always been explicit. To rule otherwise would damage the generality of the schema that covers empirical, necessary and evaluative.

How much does it count against the very possibility of a would-be vindicatory explanation, given along these lines, that someone other than Wilberforce or Clarkson could have categorized the practice we call slavery as a commercial practice (indeed many British and Americans did so categorize it and even some West Africans did) and could then have described it as 'wasteful but profitable'? Well, the first thing to say is that nothing prevents someone from seeing the practice we call slavery both as slavery *and* as a commercial practice. What is more, seeing it as a commercial practice scarcely exempts one, once the question of morality arises, from seeing it as exploitative and unjust – or indeed as slavery.

In 'Moral Cognitivism, Moral Relativism and Motivating Moral Beliefs', I wrote:

> The non-cognitivist may ask how the cognitivist could show that just anyone who is willing to take up the point of view that shall be common between one person and another *must* subsume the

institution of slavery under the concepts it is subsumed under in the argument for its injustice and insupportability. My answer to this question is that, in order to make this into a real difficulty, the opponent would have to show the workability of the scheme of moral ideas that dispenses, in the face of the phenomena such as the slave trade and its historical effects, with ideas like 'justice', 'slavery', 'using human beings as means, not ends'. When the opponent looks for those reasons, he will discover that the workability of moral ideas cannot be judged idea by idea but only by comparing systems that make use of the idea with whole systems that dispense with it – comparisons that are complex and difficult for the defenders of moral positions and equally difficult for critics who criticize in good faith.

I think I still go along with that. Is there for one who takes up the moral point of view any other possible categorization of these practices? That is the question. It is the question to be decided.

Ethical Objectivism is not true *a priori*. But if we study the dialectical resources that are available in moral argument, then we may begin to satisfy ourselves that, at least in some cases, there is (or can be put together) most or all of what is needed to show that there is no other categorization to employ and nothing else to think about the thing so categorized. Or we may not be able to satisfy ourselves of this. The question is not to be resolved *a priori*. I agree with Williams that it is not resolved by *a priori* considerations about truth. It is of the essence of Ethical Objectivism that the decision about it depends on the strength of moral *deixis*, argument and persuasion. Until we study and review the resources actually and potentially available to those who attempt to create moral conviction, we shall not know what to say about them. But *a priori* considerations about the connections between truth, objectivity, cumulative conclusiveness and vindicatory explanation do serve to suggest what we shall need to look for – simultaneously with attending to all the questions attaching to the other marks of plain truth.

Postscript II

I come now to Crispin Wright's discussion of ethical realism and anti-realism. Is the form of objectivism that I try here to formulate and then speculate how to defend a form of ethical anti-realism? And how would such a defence compare with Wright's advocacy of anti-realist truth in ethics?

In the same paper that I cited in response to Williams, I was at some pains to disentangle and keep apart the realism/anti-realism question and the two questions that I was concerned with, namely how to formulate ethical cognitivism with proper neutrality and how best to test or evaluate it. I doubted then that there was any distinctive understanding to be gained of the nature of morality or of moral judgements from allowing the emphases of the realist/anti-realist debate to affect the way one should read the questions we need to debate about ethical knowledge, objectivity, etc.

I still have this doubt: but I should emphasise that, in harbouring the doubt, I am not doubting the value of a study of the nature of the 'correctness' property φ – the property of truth if φ is indeed truth – as φ inheres or fails to inhere among the judgements of ethics. Nor am I doubting that such a study should be undertaken with a view to determining the resemblance or approximation of φ in ethics to truth in geography or geology. Indeed, such a study of φ coincides precisely with the line of inquiry which in 1976, when some anti-realists were still speaking of 'dethroning truth', I proposed in 'Truth, Invention and the Meaning of Life'.[8] Wright and I share an interest in this line of inquiry and there is a measure of convergence in the conclusions we have come to. See his *Truth and Objectivity*[9] and my *Needs, Values, Truth*, ch. 4. The thing I wanted to deprecate in my paper 'Moral Cognitivism, Moral Relativism and Motivating Moral Beliefs' was one's allowing either realist or anti-realist preconceptions to affect the conduct of the inquiry. I thought that the fruitful dichotomies and bifurcations, if there were any, ought to discover themselves in the course of the inquiries themselves, which ought not to recycle old metaphysical fixations or generalise again from the special concerns that (once upon a time) animated one striking but special disagreement in the philosophy of mathematics.

So much for the reasons I had then to seek to keep the realism/anti-realism question at arm's length from the question of ethical cognitivism. I still think these reasons may have had force. But I

[8] See *Proceedings of British Academy*, LXII, 1976, p. 354. See also 'Truth and Interpretation', *Proceedings of the Fourth International Wittgenstein Symposium*, Leinfellner, Haller, Hubner, Weingartner (eds.), (Vienna: Holder Pichler Tempsky, 1980). In his book most of the remarks that Wright makes about what I have said about truth and truth and morality are conditioned by his wish to bend each one of the claims I make into the shape of a realist thesis or a concession to anti-realism. I have never accepted the terms of this dispute.

[9] Cambridge, MA: Harvard University Press, 1992. In this book most of the remarks that Wright makes about what I have said about truth and truth and morality are conditioned by his wish to bend each one of the claims I make into the shape of a realist thesis or a concession to anti-realism. I have never accepted the terms of this dispute.

feel even more certain that the emphases and contrasts we need in order to make progress will not be generated by the kinds of denial that Wright deploys to give us an idea of what he himself would want to mean by truth in ethics. He says 'to ascribe truth to a statement need not be to ascribe a property of intrinsic meta-physical *gravitas*'. 'Intrinsic metaphysical gravitas' sounds heavy and bad. So no doubt the reader who wants to avoid it (if only because he doesn't really know what it is) is reassured to find that what he will be offered is truth in ethics without that – and without his even needing to understand what intrinsic metaphysical *gravitas* is. But this gives no positive understanding.

What then, more positively, *does* bare truth require in a sentence, according to Wright? The sentence must satisfy certain syntactic requirements (such as being subject to negation, imbedding and the rest) and it must be answerable to acknowledged standards of warrant – a substantial requirement about which all non-deflationists can agree. The satisfaction of these standards will suffice, albeit defeasibly, to justify the claim of truth. Wright spells out this general conception of truth in some further principles or platitudes. Then he says that there is no more to the property of truth than can be gathered from these platitudes. But, given that he does not complete the list and given that the platitudes themselves might *unfold* into something very demanding indeed, we may still be in doubt about what is so distinctively anti-realist in the conception of truth he has offered. And in that case, we may still be in doubt about what we should expect truth to amount to or be like in the special case of any truth that is there to be found in ethics. In which case we may be in more doubt than Wright thinks we should be about whether there is truth in ethics at all.

At this point in his paper, Wright offers the example of the funny and the incongruity of the ideas of a funniness that lies beyond all actual human responses and of a truth about that funniness. This certainly affords a further clue to what Wright thinks that truth had better not amount to in ethics. But the suggestion seems unfortunate – if only because the specifically ethical ideas of the just or the caring or the scrupulous . . . are so markedly different, and different in so many respects from the idea of the funny.

The proper response to the continuing doubt about what the anti-realist thinks truth will require and will not require in ethics might be to postpone the question of realism and anti-realism and return to the platitudes of truth themselves as Wright gives them. Maybe one should seek to develop them further for oneself. But luckily there is more information in the rest of Wright's paper about what one might expect anti-realist truth to amount to in the ethical case. He says (1) that truth in ethics will coincide with superassertibility or the durable satisfaction by a sentence of a discourse's internal disciplinary constraints; (2) that it is a language-game internal notion; (3) that truth need have nothing substantial or interesting to do with correspondence or with representation; (4) that truth in ethics is not born of facts that can contribute to the explanation of things other than moral beliefs, which is what it would need to be born of if truth were to conform to 'robustly representational conception of truth'; (5) that truth in ethics has to come to terms with the conviction expressed by so many people 'that a substantial body of the principles that inform our ordinary moral thought are essentially contestable and . . . no rational or cognitive deficiency is needed to sustain the clashes [we see within and across cultures] about things like sexual morality, the value of individual freedom, the moral status of animals and the ethics of suicide and mercy-killing'; (6) that, for truth as the moral anti-realist conceives it in ethics, 'there will be no defensible analogue of the scientific realist's thought that the real progress of science is measured by the extent to which our theories represent a reality whose nature owes nothing to our natures or the standards that inform our conception of responsible discourse about it'; (7) that the value of moral truth will be an 'instrumental, moral value, one informing better conduct'; (8) that there is nothing more for a sensible moral realist to want.

If (7) is what the anti-realist cognitivist has to say, then I think (7) will undermine (8). But perhaps (7) is not something that has to be said.

(6) has the virtue of relating in a transparent way to the intellectual origins of anti-realism (Brouwer, Dummett, etc.) while relating at the same time to a contrast that will certainly need to be marked, by anyone, between the subject matter of science and the subject matter of morality. But it is an important question whether this is a contrast at the level of sense or at the level of reference.[10] If it is a contrast at the level of sense (or content or subject matter) rather than of truth-value, then the question that remains open is whether the difference that is so well encapsulated by (6) is a difference in respect of the quality of moral judgements' *candidacy for truth*.

[10] See again 'Moral Cognitivism', § 13, paragraph two.

Something similar surely deserves to be said about (4). *Ex hypothesi*, what the acceptance of a moral judgement commits us to is the existence of a non-natural property – a property that need not pull its weight in the scientific account of the world, though it will certainly pull its weight in any account of what either affects or beckons to conscious beings. Now in fact (4) is overstated. (The courage or negligence or callousness or considerateness of a person x can make a vast difference to outcomes other than the beliefs and motives of persons. It can make a causal difference to the fate of persons either identical with x or different from x. And that which affects thought which modifies outcomes does affect outcomes.[11]) But the question is why the non-natural should not be *represented*, or *misrepresented*.

Wright's (3) is important (as is his claim, with which I agree, that correspondence and the rest are best made sense of – or I should say, can only be made sense of – derivatively from marks of truth that can be established independently of them). But, given the notorious limitations of models like the wax-impression or the photograph – limitations that apply even for such simple factual propositions as '*all* the Fs are Gs' – it is hard not to assimilate the failure Wright sees in moral realism to some universal failure in realism in general (at least as Wright glosses realism). Let me say at once that I am not going to call myself an anti-realist simply because I have long since rejected the idea that correspondence can be used to elucidate that of truth.

Here then let us move to Wright's (5). He invites the realist to come to terms with the widespread conviction that all sorts of moral question provoke disagreement which cannot be alleviated by the pointing out of any rational or cognitive shortcomings among the parties (etc.). Here, however, it seems that there is a prior question: How content should an anti-realist be, if his view is that *there is* anti-realist truth in ethics, to allow the conviction Wright speaks of to stand unchallenged and uncriticised? Is the widespread conviction Wright speaks of really consistent with truth even as the anti-realist conceives of that? For if the conviction be well considered (not merely worldly wise and time-serving), can it help but signify something profoundly gloomy about the strength of the dialectical resources of moral argument? An anti-realist truth that tolerated the situation Wright's conviction speaks of and countenanced it across the whole gamut of moral questions would

---

[11] Cf. again 'Moral Cognitivism', § 16.

scarcely be truth at all. What protects 'acknowledged standards of warrant' from the charges of inconsistency and incoherence? It is here, in the inquiry whether the said conviction is well considered, not in the elaboration of the old metaphysical metaphors, that the real work is to be done concerning the prospects for truth in ethics.

If this work were undertaken, then would it be (as Wright says) 'internal to the anti-realist camp'? I still do not understand the question well enough to agree or disagree. But maybe the notion of superassertibility, the anti-realist notion of anti-realist truth par excellence, holds the key here. See Wright's point (1) in my enumeration. The statement that *p* is superassertible if it is assertible in some state of information and then remains so *no matter how that state of information is enlarged upon or improved.* That looks like an interesting property in a statement. But at this point two difficulties lie in wait for the sincerely perplexed.

First, understanding the definition roughly and readily, one will wonder whether the truth of moral judgements (if they are ever true) could conform to this specification. What moral agents have to learn to live with is that in so many cases it is impossible to *circumscribe* the class of relevant considerations. Should one tell the truth to one who has gone off his head. (Cf. Plato, *Republic*, 331b.) Where did Orestes' duty lie to his murdered father? What was the honourable course of action for the young man mentioned in J-P. Sartre's 'Existentialism Is a Humanism' essay? How can the sense of the claim that *this* is what he should do amount to something that would be *impervious* to arbitrarily extensive increments of information?

In the second place, suppose one tries to improve one's general understanding of the definition of superassertibility. What does anti-realism make of ordinary historical facts for which all evidence is actually obliterated? (Are these facts morally neutral?) And another worry: does Wright really mean to speak of a statement's continuing to be assertible *no matter how the state of information is enlarged*? I ask because no judgement to the effect that *p* is going to stand firm despite the addition of the information that not-*p*. Or is the point meant to be that, where p is superassertible, the enlargement by not-*p* and kindred enlargements are *not available*? What then would it be for these enlargements to be unavailable? Well, they would certainly be unavailable if *p* were true. But, if that is how we have to put it, does not the finding of anti-realist truth seem to depend on the application of a non-anti-realist version of truth? Indeed the kind of generality that is involved in the definition itself of 'superassertibility' seems wholly alien to the spirit of anti-realism. Or it would seem so if only we knew otherwise than by denial what anti-realism was.

My provisional opinion is that the line of inquiry I advocate in my lecture is not anti-realist. Nor, *pace* Williams, is it very distinctively Peircean, except in respect of its fallibilist orientation upon certainty, conviction and knowledge and in respect of the highly important, if unfamiliar, Peircean idea that the creation of conviction and the achievement of conclusiveness can be cumulative.

New College
University of Oxford
Oxford OX1 3BN
England

IV

SUBJECT-IVE AND OBJECTIVE

Peter Railton

I

Morality is different – but how? Moral judgement certainly differs in various ways from ordinary judgement about the garden-variety objects in the world around us. A distinguished line of philosophers have argued that these differences are crystallised in a difference in the very nature and function of moral language. And yet grammar textbooks make no mention of a systematic distinction between moral and non-moral language, even at the level of deep structure. Indeed, moral language does not in its grammatical or logical behaviour betray the least sign of being anything other than ordinary.

Increasingly, philosophers are inclined to take this at face value. Moral judgements, for example, are held to make assertions that can be true or false in our ordinary sense of these terms. Increasingly, too, philosophers are inclined to accept all the platitudes that follow from this. Thus, since 'truth is correspondence to the facts', moral truth is correspondence to the facts, too. Ordinary discourse supports us here: 'The fact is that I've promised to go and so I'm obliged to be there' is not a quirky way of expressing oneself. It even is deemed harmless to countenance talk of 'moral properties' (in ordinary speech one would more likely hear 'moral qualities') and 'moral facts' ('moral circumstances'). This sort of talk seems to assume nothing about whether such properties or facts are *sui generis*, for example.

Perhaps, then, morality is different but moral discourse as such is not. And perhaps our willingness to talk in terms of moral properties and facts simply registers our readiness to apply the terms 'true' and 'false' to moral judgements. As such, it might be considered innocent of any significant metaphysical implications. Its real basis would be seen as lying in our discursive practices in morality, our tendencies to deliberate and disagree in distinctive ways – to make arguments, to insist upon consistency, to adduce evidence, and so on. Beyond this, no purported insight into the real composition of the world is claimed.

If moral judgement is therefore factual in a thorough-going but mundane sense, where might the supposed difference between moral judgements and ordinary worldly judgements lie?

Let us consider a recent suggestion. It is one thing to judge, another to reify the object of judgement. We must always be on guard when analysing language – moral and non-moral alike – against gratuitous reification. Sometimes reification strikes us as quite appropriate. For example, most of us are realists about the external world of mid-sized physical objects, about other minds, and about the past. But many find reification and realism suspect in other domains that nonetheless are typically accepted as factual – mathematics, modality, universals, and so on.

The question of realism vs. anti-realism has therefore seemed to some a promising way to understand how morality might be different even though moral discourse is factual. There is, after all, a lot of ground between recognising that a discourse is factual and adopting a realist attitude toward the substantives and properties occurring in it.[1] First, there is always the possibility that a *non-literal* interpretation of these terms will seem most appropriate: philosophical behaviourists argue, for example, that mental statements are equivalent to claims about actual and possible behaviour. This translation would preserve the cognitive grammar of mentalistic discourse and yield a domain of potential psychological facts, but it would hardly deserve the name 'mental (or psychological) realism'. Second, there is the further possibility that an *error theory* about the discourse will seem on reflection most appropriate: moral statements when literally interpreted, might be seen as making claims or presuppositions – such as the existence of a teleological 'natural order' – that simply never hold true in the actual world.[2] In error theories we encounter a form of anti-realism that owes nothing to a non-factualist or non-literal interpretation of moral language.

Many philosophers, however, want neither of these options. They want to say that they find at least some substantive moral judgements, literally understood, to be true. Chattel slavery is unjust. The infliction of pain upon others for one's own amusement is wrong.[3] Yet some of these same philosophers want to counten-

---

[1] I am indebted here to Gideon Rosen. See P. Railton and G. Rosen, 'Realism', in J. Kim and E. Sosa (eds.), *The Blackwell Companion to Metaphysics* (Oxford: Blackwell, 1994).

[2] The best-known example of an error theory in the moral case is that of J. L. Mackie, *Ethics: Inventing Right and Wrong* (London: Penguin, 1977).

[3] It is not important here whether we understand these judgements as absolute or *prima facie*. Even a moral realist can, for example, espouse a theory of *prima facie* moral reasons, or a

ance moral facts only so far – in particular, they wish to distance themselves from moral realism.

One way to avoid moral metaphysics while accepting the idea that at least some moral judgements, literally interpreted, are true would be to adopt non-literalism about truth itself (at least as it figures in moral discourse). But this option has already been foreclosed in our present discussion, since we are supposing that when the term 'truth' is employed in moral discourse it has its familiar sense, the same sense in which it figures in discourse about those parts of the world toward which we more readily adopt a realist attitude. Moreover, if there is a difference of metaphysical interest between moral facts and facts about garden-variety objects, we have been assuming, this is not because 'fact' has a different meaning in the two cases.[4]

Let us call *Literal Truth* the position that at least some substantive moral statements, taken literally, are literally true. What space remains between Literal Truth and moral realism?[5] Perhaps the space is only rhetorical – there is nothing a moral realist could legitimately want beyond what is contained in Literal Truth. That would be reminiscent of a familiar realist/anti-realist dialectic in which the anti-realist places the burden upon the realist to say what more could be at stake. But in this case the dialectic is different. For here it seems as if the party with the stronger interest in showing there to be something genuine at issue is not the realist (who accepts Literal Truth as a matter of course) but the moral-anti-realist-who-nonetheless-accepts-Literal-Truth. This sort of anti-realist wants to be able to distinguish morality from areas of inquiry that he thinks to be more properly informative about the shape of the real world.

A qualification is in order. Given the (uncontroversial) super-venience of moral discourse, to insist that at least some moral judgements, literally interpreted, are true is to commit oneself to

---

theory that involves vagueness and indeterminacy. We cannot saddle the moral realist with standards of absoluteness or 'rational determinacy' we do not impose upon such 'hard' domains of inquiry as biology or geology. (Just which genetic change made for the first member of *Mammalia*?) Indeed, it is commonly argued in philosophy of science that the choice of a fundamental physical theory is not 'rationally determinate', even given ideal evidence.

[4] Obviously, it would not help at this point to embrace a global anti-realism about factual discourse, since precisely the idea is to work out when a realist attitude toward a factual domain of discourse is sensible and when not.

[5] None, according to some commentators. See for example G. Sayre-McCord's introduction to his *Essays on Moral Realism* (Ithaca: Cornell University Press, 1989).

the existence in the real world – where else? – of some or other non-moral states of affairs in virtue of which the moral judgements hold. So Literal Truth by itself commits one to the idea that moral discourse reveals something of the shape of the real world after all: the world must be such as to underwrite at least some bona fide moral facts.

That could be very metaphysically informative – or not – depending upon the substantive content of moral claims, a question that cannot be bracketed in discussions of the significance of Literal Truth and that we ourselves cannot any longer postpone. One potential attraction of a position that combines Literal Truth with anti-realism about morality is that it might provide a way of capturing what has seemed to many right about emotivism while avoiding the imputation of a non-standard grammar to moral discourse and the attendant exaggerated attention to non-cognitive states. Emotivists explained the fact/value distinction by arguing that moral discourse has a grammatically *subjective* character – unlike ordinary objectual discourse it functions primarily to express the speaker's emotions rather than to describe states of affairs. Philosophers who combine Literal Truth with anti-realism will reject this grammatical way of accommodating the subjective aspect of moral discourse and the associated view of value claims as non-factual. But they can adopt the emotivists' re-orientation of moral philosophy away from the idea that moral judgement passively reports objectual states worthy of reification and toward the idea that it essentially involves the reactions and actions of subjects. This re-orientation should inhibit reification and realism, even if one grants Literal Truth. By contrast, various judgements purporting to describe the external world, other minds, and the past can be made seemingly without any necessary engagement on our part as subjects, which explains why reification and realism come much more naturally to them in the wake of Literal Truth.

Consider in this light what two philosophers have said recently about what realism would appear to involve in the moral case. John Rawls characterizes the realist's conception of moral inquiry as:

> the search for moral truth interpreted as fixed by a prior and independent order of objects and relations, whether natural or divine, an order apart and distinct from how we conceive ourselves.[6]

[6] Rawls, 'Kantian Constructivism in Moral Theory', *Journal of Philosophy* 77 (1980), p. 519. Note also the discussion in his more recent book, *Political Liberalism* (New York: Columbia University Press, 1993), lecture 3.

And in a similar vein, Crispin Wright writes in concluding a discussion of moral realism using a comparison with realism in science:

> [according to the realist] the real progress of science is measured by the extent to which our theories represent a reality whose nature owes nothing to our natures or the standards that inform our conception of reasonable discourse about it.[7]

If a realist conception of moral facts must be one in which they are 'prior and independent', or 'a reality whose nature owes nothing to our natures', then it would be clear why space remains between Literal Truth and moral realism: an anti-realist could claim that moral facts lack the metaphysical independence from human subjectivity that would sustain a realist attitude toward them. This would not be a defect in the moral facts themselves, but rather a ground for recognising that realist reification is not always licensed by a willingness to speak literally of truth and fact.

The question now becomes: Does a realist attitude necessarily bring with it a commitment to this sort of metaphysical independence?

II

Certainly some forms of realism do owe their distinctive character to this sort of commitment. Such paradigms of realism as realism about the external world, realism about the theoretical entities of natural science, and Platonism about mathematical objects have as a central component the idea that the entities or properties posited are 'prior to and independent of' any condition or experience of subjects. In that sense, they are radically non-subjective. Since 'subjective' is a notoriously slippery term, let us coin the technical term 'subject-ive' (with a hyphen) to express the notion of that which is essentially connected with the existence or experiences of subjects, i.e., beings possessing minds and points of view, being capable of forming thoughts and intentions. These paradigms of realism are, in our hiccoughing neologism, radically nonsubject-ive.

Similarly, many paradigm forms of *anti*-realism take the subject-ive as their point of departure: phenomenalists interpret physical object language in terms of actual or possible observations; observationalists do the same with the theoretical language of

---

[7] Wright, *Truth and Objectivity* (Cambridge: Harvard University Press, 1992), p. 200.

science; conventionalists trace the nature of numbers as well as the force of the logical 'must' to the practices of the mathematical community; nominalists see universals as linguistic rather than metaphysical; and atheists treat God as a mere idealisation of human characteristics ('The secret of the Holy Family is the human family', according to the Feuerbachian). It should be emphasised, however, that subject-ive does not mean subjective, at least insofar as that term is used derogatorily to suggest a domain without standards, where arbitrary opinion takes the place of judgement. Phenomenalists and observationalists have character-istically emphasised such standards of epistemic objectivity as intersubjective agreement and reliance upon rational credence functions. What these views reject in realism is not its interest in objectivity, but (what we might call) its tendency toward objectivity – its reification of a domain as independent of sub-ject-ivity.

Radical nonsubject-ivity, where it can sensibly be sustained, does help to secure several seeming hallmarks of realist thought. If a domain of entities and properties D is independent of experience, for example, then it has at least three interesting kinds of explanatory potential. First, it can in principle support non-circular explanations of the patterns in our experience – we see a tree in the quad because one is there, and not vice versa. This corresponds to a certain notion of univocal 'order of explanation'.[8] Second, D can in principle support explanations unmediated by any sort of experience – a tree falling unnoticed in the quad nonetheless leaves an elongated depression in the earth. This, taken together with the first, establishes an impressive 'width of cosmological role' for D.[9] And third, these two kinds of explanatory potential enable us to see clearly how explanations invoking the properties and entities of D can in principle pass an 'Attitude Test' of a kind suggested by Gilbert Harman: if we were to replace reference to these properties and entities in our explanations with reference only to our attitudes about D combined with associated non-D facts, genuine explanatory information would be lost.[10]

---

[8] Compare the discussion of 'order of determination' and its relation to realism, in the essays by M. Johnston and C. Wright in J. Haldane and C. Wright (eds.), *Reality, Representation and Projection* (Oxford: Oxford University Press, 1992).

[9] This useful term is due to Crispin Wright. See his *Truth and Objectivity*, ch. 5.

[10] See the discussion in ch. 1 of G. Harman, *The Nature of Morality* (New York: Oxford University Press, 1977). The notion of 'explanatory information' is roughly this: information about what a comprehensive explanatory history would contain. For discussion, see P. Railton, 'Probability, Explanation, and Information', *Synthese* 48 (1981).

(Contrast the atheist's view of religious explanations: world history has been affected in countless ways by religious belief and practice, and religious conviction has led many to have experiences which they call miracles or sensations of the presence of God, but no actual deity has ever caused any perception or even the swerving of a single atom. For the atheist, then, if religious explanations were replaced systematically with explanation in terms of religious attitudes and collateral non-religious phenomena, no genuine explanation would be left out. The theistic realist, by contrast, would insist that in many cases no such explanatory replacement is possible.) These three notions of explanatory potential give us an idea of the particular sort of explanatory pay-off that positing a domain of nonsubject-ive entities and properties can yield, and which might well make such a posit worthwhile.

It is natural to associate realism with this sort of radical nonsubject-ivity. The realist is said to want entities and properties that are 'out there' in the world, independent of the projections of our beliefs and indifferent to the tossings and turnings of our imaginations – entities and properties that are there *anyway*.[11] This association bodes ill for the moral case. We have a degree of confidence – perhaps even justified confidence? – that we have some idea of what it would be like for rocks and trees, quasars and molecules, heat and mean molecular kinetic energy to be 'prior to and independent of' all subject-ivity. By contrast, the very idea that there might be a realm of moral properties subsisting independent of all subject-ive phenomena – all facts about human nature or experience, say – would be philosophical adventurism of the first order. Thus interpreted, moral realism is a non-starter.

III

But is this train of thought compelling? It overlooks the seeming platitude that the nature of realism about any domain depends upon the nature of that domain itself. What do we imagine the entities or properties of this domain to be like? If there were such things, what would they do? The question of realism about a domain D of purported entities and properties cannot be treated in a purely generic way – we must ask more specifically what would it take to fill D's bill.

Let us try to make this platitudinous thought more explicit.

---

[11] I owe this phrase to Gideon Rosen.

Suppose we were, for a given domain D, to draw up a 'job description' for purported D-entities or D-properties – 'D's' for short – based upon our ordinary notions, folk theories as influenced by scientific developments, relatively uncontroversial applications, paradigm cases, and so on.[12] This job description is to be very literal-minded, that is, it attempts to express what D's *if literally understood* are supposed to be and do.

For example, a job description for *physical object* would include not only such minimal conditions as spatio-temporal location and continuity, but also all manner of humdrum activities and folk-scientific functions. Thus physical objects persist when unobserved; they non-circularly explain various features of our sensory experience; they have properties which enjoy a certain independence from our conceptions of them; and they include, as paradigms, rocks and trees; and so on. The presence in our intuitive job description for physical objects of these various elements is reflected in the fact that almost everyone views phenomenalism as a *revisionary* or non-literal account of our physical object discourse.

Job descriptions therefore are hardly free of folk-theorising. As we noted earlier, mental states are commonsensically supposed to be internal conditions of sentient beings that non-circularly explain their manifest behaviour. Analytic behaviourism thus is widely seen as a revisionary account of our mentalistic discourse. The Christian God is supposed to be a person-like entity with

---

[12] This way of approaching things is obviously inspired by the Ramsey-Carnap-Lewis approach to defining theoretical terms. (See, e.g., D. Lewis, 'How to Define Theoretical Terms', reprinted in his *Philosophical Papers*, vol. 1 [New York: Oxford University Press, 1989].) Unlike the classic forms of this approach, however, there is no assumption here that the job description will be 'observational' in the sense of being innocent of 'theoretical' predicate constants. Moreover, as in Lewis's more recent versions of this approach, it is assumed that the job description is modified by a qualifier to the effect that entities or properties can meet the description more or less fully.

Lewis himself does not offer this sort of account of moral terms (see his 'Dispositional Theories of Value', *Proceedings of the Aristotelian Society* suppl. vol. 63 [1989]), preferring a more explicit definition. Defending a Ramsey-Carnap-Lewis approach to a class of terms requires that the corresponding properties purport to have the right sort and extent of theoretical roles. Certainly this can be doubted in the moral case. I would argue that moral discourse is well-integrated into our folk explanatory theories, which include counterfactual-supporting generalisations linking needs and wants, goods and functions, virtues and stable personality traits, and rightness and social functionality (see for example the discussion in P. Railton, 'Moral Realism', *Philosophical Review* 87 (1986) and 'Naturalism and Prescriptivity', *Social Philosophy and Policy* 7 (1989)). These theories attempt to explain, among other things, both why we sometimes arrive at moral knowledge or act well and why we sometimes do not.

extraordinary powers. An interpretation of 'God exists' as 'I hereby commit myself to loving my neighbour' would, I suspect, strike most theists as non-literal.

Some elements of job descriptions are more epistemic in character. In the case of mental states, we take ourselves to have a kind of access to at least some of our own mental states that is more direct than our access to the mental states of others. In the case of physical objects, we take ourselves to know something of them through experience. In the case of numbers, too, we take ourselves to know something of them, but with a special kind of certainty, and through means seemingly quite unlike those of ordinary observation. A radically empiricist interpretation of mathematics, like Mill's, is to some degree epistemically revisionary.

But to be revisionary is not to be wrong. Ordinary discourse is bound to contain not only vagueness and ambiguity, but inconsistencies, incoherences, impossibilities. Ordinary discourse shows the sedimentation and metamorphosis of centuries of folk, scientific, and quasi-scientific thought, and any account free of ambiguity and incoherence is bound to be somewhat revisionary. Job descriptions are literal, but it seldom is possible that they be literally met when fully spelled out. They are meant to map out explicitly the intuitive landscape toward which philosophical accounts are directed, alternatively claiming with pride to capture large tracts of terrain or arguing defensively that those parts they cannot fit are best got rid of.

Any such attempt at explicitness about what is uncontroversial is itself of course bound to be somewhat controversial, especially around the edges. Just *how* folk – as opposed to scientifically informed – a conception do we follow? And just *which* folk do we consult? Common sense is not regimented or homogenous. Consider 'freedom of the will'. It certainly appears to be part of our commonsense conception of free will that free agents could have acted otherwise. But is it part of this conception – or a philosophical invention meant to explain it – that agents are able to act contra-causally? Moreover, in some languages the commonsense term is closer to 'free choice' than 'free will'. Does our folk conception of free action involve commitment to the will as a little piece of machinery turning the psychic gears inside the agent? Or would a belief-desire-based model of choice more typical of contemporary psychology suffice?[13] It will always be an essential

---

[13] I am grateful here to Jean-Pierre Dupuy.

part of revisionist strategy to claim that what seems to some to be part of the intuitive landscape is really a mirage or a philosophical excrescence.

IV

With these caveats about 'reading off' job descriptions from common sense or expecting them to be fully met in mind, let us ask what the job listing for moral properties might look like. This is a fairly broad terrain, including properties as diverse as those of obligation, value, and character. To give the full listing would involve a large number of more or less interdependent job descriptions. Moreover, moral properties are asked to do a lot of things. We cite them in deliberation, assessment, interpretation, instruction, punishment, prediction, and explanation. Their job descriptions would be complex, and much intertwined with other elements of commonsense thought. A moral realist need not be non-revisionary with respect to the whole lot. And a moral realist need not be a realist about the whole lot. Just as one can be a scientific realist about entities and events but not about probability or nomic necessity, one can be a moral realist about value and virtue but not duty and rights.

Let us focus herein on questions of moral value and evaluation (rather than claims about moral duty, say), and pay special attention initially to some questions about explanation that have figured centrally in recent discussions of moral realism. And let us remember our larger purpose. Literal Truth about a domain D is committed to the idea that the job descriptions of enough central D entities or properties are sufficiently well met by conditions in the actual world to enable us to formulate some substantive truths about D's as literally understood. Realism in turn involves Literal Truth. Does it necessarily involve a further demand that the entities and properties of D be of an independent or nonsubject-ive nature?

Consider first the realist about the external world of physical objects. Our ordinary conception of physical objects has it that they affect not only consciously-formulated beliefs ('I think we've struck a submerged reef') but also experiential states of a kind prior to conceptualised belief ('We test to see if the newborn can follow a flashlight with his eyes'), non-experiential states of subjective beings ('I always get freckles like this in the summer sun'), and radically nonsubject-ive states ('The earth's gravitational field holds the moon in its orbit').[14] As we noted earlier, it is all part of a day's work for physical objects to have effects in the world unmediated by and independent of any conscious or subject-ive state. An interpretation of physical object discourse bold enough to deny this would be bound to be viewed as too revisionary to vindicate our ordinary notion.

For this reason, nonsubject-ivity belongs to the job description of physical objects, and therefore is as much a commitment of Literal Truth about physical object discourse as it is an implication of realism about physical objects. To believe that at least some physical object statements, literally understood, are literally true, is not to accept any particular explanatory claims (except perhaps, with the usual qualifications, for paradigm cases). But it is to accept the existence of entities with this sort of explanatory potential as part of the furnishings of the actual world.

Contrast the case of belief. Common sense has it that beliefs are the possessions of subjects, and never found in their absence. One would not know what to make of a demand that beliefs as such, as ordinarily understood, have an explanatory role in the cosmos independent of all consciousness and unmediated by thought or its embodiment. The chief explanatory roles figuring in the job description of belief concern the shaping of thought, inference, action, perception, expectation, emotion, dreams, and so on. The effects of beliefs on the wider, nonsubject-ive world are always mediated by these states and processes and their embodiment in subject-ive beings. To be sure, their embodiment itself can have unmediated effects on the nonsubject-ive world. The pattern of electrical activation of my neurons as I ponder how to turn a key in a stubborn lock subtly affects the electromagnetic field surrounding me. But beliefs 'in their own right' – beliefs as such rather than their embodying conditions – effect changes in the physical world only indirectly, thanks to their influential role in the lives of the subjects wherein they reside.

A requirement that beliefs constitute a 'prior and independent order' or possess a 'wide cosmological role' would thus certainly not be part the conditions for Literal Truth about belief discourse. Might it be an additional condition necessary to move from Literal Truth to realism? Could a non-eccentric realist about belief afford to be so eccentrically nonsubject-ive about the nature of belief? In

---

[14] This brief list follows Wright's description of 'wide cosmological role' in *Truth and Objectivity*, pp. 196–99.

principle, a realist can espouse a tolerable revisionism, bending our ordinary conceptions in order to obtain a good enough fit overall. Yet it is hard to see what positive contribution would be made to the vindication of commonsense or scientific belief discourse by attempting to introduce beliefs without believers.

More generally, it need be no part of the ambition of realism about a domain of discourse D to attribute to the entities or properties in D causal-explanatory roles or conditions that go beyond the roles and paradigm cases found among the 'job listings' of D. Of course, any given realist might insist upon such further roles in order to meet other philosophical desiderata. A naturalist might insist as a condition for a realist attitude toward D that a naturalistic reduction of D's be in the offing, or that D's win their way into our best scientific theories rather than remain at the level of commonsense explanatory frameworks. But this naturalistic condition would be a specific way of being a realist or motivating realism, not a requisite of realism in general. And no matter what stripe of realism is in question, it will tend to complicate the realist's life to insist upon a role or standing for D's that goes against the grain of the job listings for D. A starkly object-ivist view of so paradigmatically subject-ive a phenomenon as belief might more appropriately be viewed as a replacement theory rather than a form of realism. Similarly, the contemporary scientist who says that God is, for him, simply the laws of physics themselves is more likely to be seen as offering a substitute for traditional notions of God than a vindication of them.

If we are to make sense of the question of realism about belief, then there must be a way of being a realist about subject-ive domains. But what of the notion that realism about a domain D is distinguished by its commitment to the 'objective' status of D's? Is there nothing to this? Or, could there be so little to realism?

Beliefs are fundamentally subject-ive, given their jobs, but it must be kept in mind that the sense of 'subject-ive' is technical and stipulative. It is opposed not to 'objective', but to 'object-ive', that is, having to do essentially with nonsubject-ive entities – entities that lack a mind or point of view, entities that are not a locus of experience or intention. Knowledge, for example, is by its nature subject-ive since it involves belief. But though it therefore cannot be object-ive, it might well be objective. And so might belief and belief-attribution. Consider the 'Attitude Test' mentioned earlier.[15]

---

[15] There are numerous dimensions to our none-too-well-understood notion of objectivity. Here we will be concerned mostly with those aspects reflected in the Attitude Test. For a

Can we uniformly replace the purported explanatory role of beliefs by reference instead to what we take ourselves to believe, without any loss of explanation? Or does belief have the potential to support explanations even in the face of what we take ourselves to believe? According to a familiar strain of anti-realism about belief, there are no facts about what we believe which obtain 'outside' an interpretive scheme, so that the whole contribution of belief-talk to understanding human behaviour can be captured by talking instead of belief-attributions, norms of belief-attribution, and so on. Realists about belief, on the contrary, think that there are facts about what an individual believes that can contribute to the explanation of his behaviour in ways not dependent upon his interpretive scheme or ours.

Realists here take their cue in part from commonsense thought about belief. We earlier noted that belief is commonsensically treated as an internal state of individuals that has a causal or quasi-causal role in shaping their conduct, sometimes consciously sometimes not. If common sense is right about belief, then belief attributions and interpretive schemes are answerable to facts about the distribution of beliefs, not the other way around. Belief discourse would pass the Attitude Test and, to that extent, possess a kind of objectivity. Because its explanatory role is always mediated by subjects, belief has narrow explanatory scope; but because this role is not always mediated by self-conception or interpretation, belief can be an objective feature of the subject-ive part of the world. Philosophical approaches to belief that treat belief as radically indeterminate and interpretation-dependent deny that belief possesses this sort of objectivity, and therefore strike the man in the street as quite a novelty (at least in my experience), surprisingly at odds with a literal understanding what beliefs are supposed to be. Indeed, such approaches collide with our ordinary way of speaking of ourselves in profound ways, and even flirt with incoherence.[16]

What, then of the moral case? If moral value were a something rather than a nothing, what sort of a something would it be? And

fuller description of some notions of objectivity, see P. Railton, 'Marxism and Scientific Objectivity', reprinted in R. Boyd, P. Gasper, and J. D. Trout (eds.), *The Philosophy of Science* (Cambridge: MIT Press, 1991).

[16] For relevant discussion of the possible incoherence of another sort of denial of Literal Truth about belief discourse, see P. Boghossian, 'The Status of Content', *Philosophical Review* 99 (1989).

what would it do, or help to explain? What would its paradigm
cases be? Although it is no ambition of this paper to sketch out a
complete idea of the job description of any moral property, we do
need to ask: Would moral value be subject-ive, like belief? And, if
so, would it be capable of (at least) the same sort of objectivity as
belief?

It certainly seems safe to say that moral value has essentially to
do with subjects. Just as a world altogether without conscious
beings would contain no beliefs, so would it lack moral phenomena.
The development of moral philosophy throughout the modern
period has been deeply influenced by Hume's observation of a
special connection between moral evaluation and action, and by
Kant's insistence that moral reasoning must be practical. The
exact nature and modality of the connections between moral
thought and the experience or agency of subjects are matters of
continuing controversy within moral philosophy. But it is relatively
uncontroversial that commonsense moral discourse supposes there
to be some such connections – e.g., that 'ought' implies 'can' and
that evaluation is normally associated with motivation – and that
any satisfactory account of morality must somehow accommodate
or otherwise explain these ties. We have numerous paradigm cases
of moral value or rightness, but so far as I know none that concern
wholly nonsubject-ive phenomena.[17]

Since the job description is subject-ive in this way, there can be
no question of Literal Truth or realism about moral properties as
requiring a 'prior and independent order'. Yet, according to either
realism or Literal Truth, moral properties might nonetheless
possess the sort of objectivity we found in the case of belief.

Consider some examples of commonsense moral explanations.
The injustice of segregation helps explain why it produced
widespread alienation and discontent and an eventual movement
for change. The honest decency of a colleague helps explain why
she has come to be listened to with some care in controversial
matters. The deviousness of a parent helps explain the insecurity of
his child later in life. And so on. Such explanations are rough but
informative. For example, we learn something when an observer
attributes an important role in explaining a country's repeated

---

[17] This is not true of value discourse in general. Even if aesthetic value must in the end be
understood as somehow a relational matter involving subjects, still, many paradigm cases of
objects possessing aesthetic value are inanimate objects.

bouts of social instability to underlying injustices rather than to economic downturns or political factors alone.

Such moral explanations – at least, when offered non-metaphorically – have narrow ambitions regarding cosmic scope. Their explananda are always in the first instance features of subjects.[18] Subjects can of course go on in various ways to change the nonsubject-ive world – popular rebellions attributable in part to social injustice have, for example, led to changes in settlement patterns or agricultural practices with profound ecological effects. What matters most for our purposes, however, is that many moral explanations would pass the Attitude Test in the following sense: they could not be replaced without loss by an explanation adverting only to the moral beliefs of those involved. A social order's injustice may produce alienation and dysfunction well before any articulated sense of its injustice surfaces within the population. A parent's dishonesty may undermine the solidity of a child's sense of self long before any glimmer of a moral critique of the parent emerges in the child's mind – if indeed it ever does. These explanatory accounts are in the first instance unmediated by moral concepts or beliefs. It would be quite a different analysis of a situation to trace the origins of a child's difficulties to the acceptance of a morally-conceptualised *belief* on his part that his father is behaving deceptively.

Moral sceptics and nonfactualists will on general grounds refuse to take any moral explanation at face value, for they deny the existence of moral properties. If these purported explanations are at all informative, they will argue, it is because of what such accounts tell us indirectly about moral beliefs, accepted norms, and other non-moral conditions. But here we are addressing the philosopher who has already accepted Literal Truth in the moral case. And commonsense moral discourse, taken literally, is so thoroughly interwoven with commonsense theorising about human action, society, and history, that it seems an evident part of the full job description of moral properties for them to have various genuine explanatory roles.

No full job description for moral virtue, for example, could leave it explanatorily inert. It is of the essence of virtue that

---

[18] We set aside here, as we did in the case of belief, explanations couched entirely in terms of the conditions of *embodiment* by subjects of the properties in question. Clearly the 'subjacent base' of moral properties, as R. M. Hare has called it, can directly explain features of the world without subject-ive mediation.

possession of a virtue would help explain constancies of individual behaviour across varying circumstances, and that variations in behaviour across individuals facing similar circumstances can be attributed to the presence or absence of virtues.[19] Moreover, it is of the essence of virtue-based explanations that they are *objective* in the sense discussed above – it is one's underlying moral character, not simply one's moral beliefs (and certainly not one's beliefs about one's character), that explains one's conduct. The question of whether to accept certain moral explanations as objective therefore need not derive from concerns or reifying tendencies specific to realism at all. It is difficult to imagine acceptance of the literal truth of substantive claims involving moral virtues without acceptance of the idea that virtues afford some measure of objective explanation (at least to the extent of passing the Attitude Test).

If differences over how fully moral properties can do their purported jobs – including their purported objective explanatory jobs – belong to the space of revisionism within Literal Truth as much as they do to realism, what sorts of differences might distinguish Literal Truth from moral realism? We have already seen that they cannot be differences over the subject-ive character of moral properties – that feature of moral job descriptions is sufficiently central to be common ground to all interpretations of moral discourse with any hope of avoiding error theory. Could it be that 'realist' is simply the self-description of choice of those who think that the job descriptions of moral properties can fairly fully be met – so that adopting the position Literal Truth while rejecting the label 'moral realism' would be a way of signalling that one thinks some substantial, but still tolerable, revisionism of common sense is called for? There is something to this thought, but not, I suspect, enough. More than likely, there will be self-described moral realists who are more revisionary with respect to ordinary moral discourse than some self-styled quietists who accept Literal Truth but balk at moral realism.

Differences about the appropriateness of an attitude of realism toward the moral among those accepting Literal Truth will, I suspect, lie less in matters about whether to accept at face value

---

[19] These features of discourse about moral virtue testify both the empirical content and the empirical vulnerability of moral explanation. At least one important tendency in contemporary psychology is sceptical about the existence of continuing traits of character capable of explaining patterns of constancies and variability in individual conduct across situations. See L. Ross and R. Nisbett, *The Person and the Situation* (Philadelphia: Temple University Press, 1994), esp. ch. 4.

moral explanations than in general interpretive questions about the metaphysical weight of terms like 'cause', 'explain', 'property', and 'objective'. In any event, our concern about whether the job descriptions of moral properties – including the explanatory elements – can be met does not itself depend upon any 'heavyweight' notion of 'explain' or 'property'. What is at issue here is a matter common to Literal Truth and realism: whether a large constellation of platitudes, commonsensical practices, folk notions, imported scientific theorising, and paradigm cases can – to a tolerable degree – be found to be instantiated in this world.

V

Given the differences in job listings between the domain of physical objects and the moral domain, it is unsurprising that moral judgement is a different business from ordinary judgement about objects in the world around us. Moral properties could hardly do their job if they were radically object-ive, physical objects could hardly do their job if they were not.

Belief furnishes us a model of how there can be a genuine issue of realism and objectivity concerning a subject-ive domain. But in emphasising the parallel between moral realism and realism about belief, I do not mean to suggest that moral realism must be a form of psychologism. For commonsense moral thought includes various roles for moral properties that are not obviously psychological. Most notably, there are the so-called *normative* roles of moral notions – the action-guiding character of terms like 'ought', 'must', and 'good'. It is an open question whether any purely psychological theory can give an account of this normativity.

Yet here, too, an interesting parallel with belief holds. For it is also an open question whether any purely psychological theory can give an account of belief. Beliefs are commonsensically attributed propositional content as well as causal roles. Moreover, these contents have correctness conditions that are commonsensically seen as objective in the sense that the content of one's beliefs is not simply a matter of what one takes it to be – it is not a matter of idiosyncratic will, free stipulation, or spontaneous creation. If the job description of belief is to be met in its central elements, an essentially subject-ive state must be capable of possessing the sort of objective normativity embodied in correctness conditions. But the puzzle here does not arise from the fact that the state is subject-ive as such. It is no more clear – on the contrary, it is a good deal less clear – how a purely nonsubject-ive state of the world could be a bearer of content. If the feat of creating and embodying states with correctness conditions can be accomplished at all, it seems evident that subjects rather than mere objects will be the ones to do it.

The puzzle is *how* they might do this: how subjects might, by doing what they do, place themselves within a normative framework that sustains a distinction between what is correct and what is done (including what is as a matter of fact taken to be correct). This is as much a puzzle in the case of belief as it is in the moral case, though not the same puzzle – morality is certainly to that extent different. And it is a puzzle for Literal Truth even apart from realism. For if moral discourse or discourse about belief is to any significant degree literally true, then somehow we subjects must have brought objective normativity into being.[20]

Philosophy Department
University of Michigan
Ann Arbor, MI 48109–1432
USA

---

[20] I would like to thank Paul Boghossian, Allan Gibbard, Paul Horwich, David Lewis, Gideon Rosen, Michael Smith, and Crispin Wright for much helpful conversation. An earlier version of this paper was presented at an NEH Summer Seminar at the University of Nebraska and at the Centre de Recherche en Epistémologie Appliquée, Ecole Polytechnique; I am grateful to those attending for many useful comments and criticisms.

V

INTERNALISM'S WHEEL

Michael Smith

If an agent judges that she morally ought to φ in certain circumstances C then, according to internalists, absent practical irrationality, she must be motivated, to some extent, to φ in C.[1] Internalists thus accept what I have elsewhere called the 'practical-ity requirement on moral judgement'.[2] Externalists deny this.[3] They hold that agents may not be motivated to any extent to act in accordance with their moral judgements, and this without any irrationality on their behalf.

Internalism has traditionally been thought to function as a high-level conceptual constraint on moral judgement, accounts of which are supposed to be assessed, *inter alia*, by the extent to which they can explain and capture its truth. Unfortunately, however, on closer inspection this doesn't amount to much in the way of a constraint. There are many different theories about the nature and content of moral judgement that aspire to explain and capture the truth embodied in internalism, and these theories share little in common beyond that aspiration.

Worse still, as I will argue in what follows, these theories are perhaps best thought of as lying around the perimeter of a wheel, much like Fortune's Wheel, with each theory that lies further on along the perimeter representing itself as motivated by difficulties that beset the theory that precedes it. The mere existence of

---

[1] See W. D. Falk ' "Ought" and Motivation', *Proceedings of the Aristotelian Society* (48) 1948; G. Harman, 'Moral Relativism Defended', *Philosophical Review* 85 (1975); J. L. Mackie, *Ethics: Inventing Right and Wrong* (Harmondsworth: Penguin, 1977); J. McDowell, 'Are Moral Requirements Hypothetical Imperatives?', *Proceedings of the Aristotelian Society* suppl. vol., 1978; M. Platts, *Ways of Meaning* (London: Routledge and Kegan Paul, 1979); S. Blackburn, *Spreading the Word* (Oxford: Clarendon Press, 1984), ch. 6; C. Korsgaard, 'Skepticism about Practical Reason', *Journal of Philosophy* 83 (1986); M. Johnston, 'Dispositional Theories of Value', *Proceedings of the Aristotelian Society* suppl. vol., 1989; M. Smith, *The Moral Problem* (Oxford: Blackwell, 1994), chs. 1, 3.

[2] Smith, *The Moral Problem*, p. 62.

[3] See W. Frankena, 'Obligation and Motivation in Recent Moral Philosophy' in A. I. Melden (ed.), *Essays on Moral Philosophy* (Seattle: University of Washington Press, 1958); P. Foot, 'Morality as a System of Hypothetical Imperatives', reprinted in her *Virtues and Vices* (Berkeley: University of California Press, 1978); P. Railton, 'Moral Realism', *Philosophical Review* 95 (1986); D. Brink, 'Externalist Moral Realism', *Southern Journal of Philosophy* suppl. vol., 1986.

Internalism's Wheel need not pose a problem for internalists, of course. They may believe that the truth about ethics lies wherever Internalism's Wheel stops spinning. But a problem evidently does arise if Internalism's Wheel is in perpetual motion, for then the truth about ethics presumably lies nowhere at all on Internalism's Wheel.

Let me now confess. I am an internalist, but an internalist who is worried, deep down, by the thought that Internalism's Wheel is indeed in perpetual motion. Since externalism too seems to me to be seriously flawed – as I have argued elsewhere, externalism is committed to an implausible moral psychology[4] – the conclusion I see looming is thus wholescale moral scepticism. Endless cycles of Internalism's Wheel augur in favour of the view that moral concerns are, quite literally, incoherent.

In sections I through V, I state the arguments against various internalist accounts of moral judgement. I describe examples of the theories that lie around Internalism's Wheel, and I explain why each of these theories is able to represent itself as motivated by problems that beset the theory that precedes it. By the end of section V we will have come full circle. Internalism will look like it is in deep trouble. But then, in section VI, I reassess this situation. I argue, though only rather tentatively, that one of the theories we considered has fewer difficulties and more advantages than the others. As I see it, if there is truth to be found in ethics at all, it is here that that truth lies.[5]

I Expressivism

Faced with theories that occupy various points around the perimeter of a wheel, it is of course quite arbitrary where we start. But let us begin with the theory whose claims about morality are most outlandish, for then the fact that we manage to argue ourselves in a circle will seem all the more remarkable. We therefore turn Internalism's Wheel to expressivism.

Like the early emotivists, expressivists tell us that when we make claims like 'A morally ought to φ in circumstances C' we are not

---

[4] See Smith, *The Moral Problem*, pp. 60–76. D. Copp discusses this argument in his 'Moral Obligation and Moral Motivation', in J. Couture and K. Nielsen (eds.), *New Essays on Metaethics, Canadian Journal of Philosophy* suppl. vol., 1996.

[5] To anticipate, the theory I defend is the non-relative version of the dispositional theory of value I argue for in *The Moral Problem*.

saying anything about the way things are, but are rather expressing certain emotions or feelings we have about the way things are to be. Our judgement is an expression of our desire that A φs in C, and perhaps also an expression of our desire that others too desire that A φs in C. This view of moral judgement has radical implications. It entails, for example, that moral claims are not truth-assessable, and that, lacking as they do any truth conditions, we must therefore give the semantics of moral claims exclusively in terms of their expressive function.

But why would anyone believe this radical view of moral judgement? In *Spreading the Word* Simon Blackburn tells us that internalism itself provides the reason.

> Evaluative commitments are being contrasted with other, truth-conditional judgements or beliefs. This contrast means that to have a commitment of this sort is to hold an attitude, not a belief, and that in turn should have implications for the explanation of people's behaviour. The standard model of explanation of why someone does something attributes both a belief and a desire to the agent. The belief that the bottle contains poison does not by itself explain why someone avoids it; the belief coupled with the normal desire to avoid harm does. So if moral commitments express *attitudes*, they should function to supplement beliefs in the explanation of action. If they express beliefs, they should themselves need supplementing by mention of desires in a fully displayed explanation of action (fully displayed because, of course, we often do not bother to mention obvious desires and beliefs, which people will presume each other to have). It can then be urged that moral commitments fall in the right way of the active, desire, side of this fence. If someone feels moral distaste or indignation at cruelty to animals, he only needs to believe that he is faced with a case of it to act or be pulled towards acting. It seems to be a conceptual truth that to regard something as good is to feel a pull towards promoting or choosing it, or towards wanting other people to feel the pull towards promoting or choosing it. Whereas if moral commitments express beliefs that certain truth-conditions are met, then they could apparently co-exist with any kind of attitude to things meeting the truth-conditions. Someone might be indifferent to things which he regards as good, or actively hostile to them.[6]

---

[6] Blackburn, *Spreading the Word*, pp. 187–88.

Simple though it might be, however, this argument raises all sorts of problems.

Internalism is the premise from which expressivism is supposed to follow. But how does Blackburn formulate this premise? He tells us that internalism is the 'conceptual truth' that 'to regard something as good is to feel a pull towards promoting or choosing it, or towards wanting other people to feel the pull towards promoting or choosing it'. But far from this being a conceptual truth, the one expressed by internalism, it is no truth at all.

The 'is' suggests a biconditional, but the biconditional is false in both directions. It is, after all, a commonplace that drug addicts, and others who are alienated from their projects, may want to promote, or want other people to promote, certain outcomes, without regarding those outcomes as good. They need not suppose that their projects have any normative significance whatsoever.[7] And it is also a commonplace that depressives, and others suffering from emotional disturbances, may regard outcomes as good which, because of their depression or emotional disturbance, they have no desire whatsoever to promote. Projects which they suppose to have normative significance may leave them unmoved.[8] Contrary to Blackburn, then, it is the case that 'someone might be indifferent to things which he regards as good, or actively hostile to them.'

Note that these examples do not undermine the truth of internalism as that doctrine was spelled out at the very beginning of this paper, however. Internalism is the view that an agent who judges something good should feel a pull towards promoting it, whether or not she does in fact. The examples are helpful, as they allow us to give commonsense content to this idea. They suggest that someone who makes moral judgements without being motivated must be suffering from compulsion, or weakness, or depression, or emotional disturbance or something similar. These constitute manifestations of practical unreason that can defeat the connection between moral judgement and motivation even if internalism is true.[9]

Once we remember that internalism posits a normative connection between moral judgement and motivation we see immediately that expressivism is unable to say anything by way of an

[7] Watson, 'Free Agency', reprinted in G. Watson (ed.), Free Will (Oxford: Oxford University Press); Smith, The Moral Problem, pp. 133–34
[8] Stocker, 'Desiring the Bad: An Essay in Moral Psychology', Journal of Philosophy 76 (1979); Smith, The Moral Problem, pp.135–36
[9] See P. Pettit and M. Smith, 'Practical Unreason', Mind (102) 1993.

explanation of it. If when an agent regards something as good she needn't be motivated at all to promote it, it cannot be the case that her regarding it as good is an expression of her motivation. At best, it seems, her judgement is the expression of a motivation she *should* have. But a motivation that should be had need not be a psychological state that even exists to be expressed. Internalism therefore seems to suggest that, contrary to expressivism, moral judgements are not expressions of motivations at all.[10]

Nor should this conclusion be surprising. There are, after all, quite independent reasons for thinking that moral judgements express beliefs rather than desires, and that the explanation of internalism should therefore concern the connection between moral belief and desire, not the constitution of moral judgement by desire. The independent reasons are familiar from the work of Peter Geach.[11] We already mentioned the fact that expressivists are committed to the view that someone who says, for example, 'It is wrong to kick cats', is not saying something that is truth-assessable. Instead, they tell us, it is as if she were saying 'Boo for kicking cats!' But, as Geach points out, this is a difficult view to maintain. After all, why do the sentences we use when we make moral judgements have so many of the features of ordinary truth-apt sentences? And why do they have so few of the features of sentences that are overtly expressive?

Consider an utterance of 'The sentence "It is wrong to kick cats" is true' by way of example. Why is it perfectly permissible to say this when it is not permissible to say 'The sentence "Boo for kicking cats!" is true'? The sentence 'Boo for kicking cats!', which is overtly

---

[10] How might expressivists reply? They might argue that moral judgements express a disposition to be motivated: a second-order desire, a desire about which first-order desires to have, not a first-order desire, a desire about what to do. They might then insist that an agent who desires that she desires that she φs in C – which is the second-order desire her judgement that she morally ought to φ in C expresses – *is* practically irrational if she doesn't desire to φ in C. But the reply is unconvincing. What the examples of heroin addiction, depression and emotional disturbance show is that the mere fact an agent desires something does not, as such, confer any special normative status on that thing. An agent may desire that she φs in C without regarding her φ-ing in C as good. The point is fully general. There is no exception for that instance of the schema where we substitute 'desiring to do something' for 'φ-ing'. A related point is made by Gary Watson in his criticisms of Harry Frankfurt's second-order desire account of freedom of the will. See Frankfurt's 'Freedom of the Will and the Concept of a Person' and Watson's 'Free Agency' both reprinted in G. Watson (ed.), *Free Will*, (Oxford: Oxford University Press, 1982). See also the explicit criticism of second-order desire accounts of weakness of will in J. Kennett, 'Decision Theory and Weakness of Will' in *Pacific Philosophical Quarterly* 72 (1991).

[11] Geach, 'Assertion', *Philosophical Review* 75 (1965).

expressive, behaves like an expressive sentence. It resists embedding in contexts, like 'The sentence "____" is true' that might
otherwise have been thought to be the exclusive preserve of truth-
assessable sentences. But the sentence 'It is wrong to kick cats'
behaves for all the world like a truth-assessable sentence rather
than an expressive sentence. It embeds in just this and other
similar contexts: 'A believes that____', 'If____then p' and so on.

Expressivists therefore face the enormous difficulty of explaining,
in expressive terms, how and why moral sentences function like
ordinary truth-apt sentences that are used to express the contents
of beliefs, rather than like overtly expressive sentences which are
used to express emotions.[12] Some expressivists, like Blackburn
himself, have confronted this task fairly and squarely. It must be
said that they have met with at best limited success, however.[13]
The fact that they have not yet come up with a convincing
explanation does not mean that no such explanation is forthcoming.
It does, however, make pessimism about their success seem
appropriate. It therefore seems wise to assume that moral sentences
express beliefs rather than desires. So Internalism's Wheel turns.

II Speaker Relativism

We are now looking for a theory that can explain two things. First,
it must give an account of what moral beliefs are beliefs about –
that is, it must give their truth conditions – and, second, it must use
that account to explain the normative connection between moral
belief and motivation. James Dreier's speaker relativism, a close
relative of expressivism, attempts just these tasks.[14]

[12] C. Wright has argued, wrongly as it seems to me, that functioning like an ordinary
truth-apt sentence is all there is to being a truth-apt sentence: see his *Truth and Objectivity*
(Cambridge, Mass: Harvard University Press, 1992). A general discussion of this issue can
be found in M. Smith, 'Why Expressivists About Value Should Love Minimalism About
Truth'; J. Divers and A. Miller, 'Why the Expressivist About Value Should Not Love
Minimalism About Truth'; P. Horwich, 'The Essence of Expressivism'; and M. Smith,
'Minimalism, Truth-Aptitude and Belief' (all in *Analysis* 54 [1994]), and in F. Jackson,
G. Oppy and M. Smith, 'Minimalism and Truth-Aptness', *Mind* 103 (1994).
[13] Blackburn's attempts can be found in his *Spreading the Word*, ch. 6; 'Attitudes and
Contents', *Ethics* 98 (1988); 'Realism, Quasi or Queasy?' in J. Haldane and C. Wright (eds.),
Reality, Representation and Projection (Oxford University Press, 1994). Decisive replies to
Blackburn can be found in B. Hale's 'The Compleat Projectivist' *Philosophical Quarterly* 36
(1986), and 'Can There Be a Logic of Attitudes?' and 'Postscript', both in Haldane and
Wright. See also C. Wright, 'Moral Values, Projection and Secondary Qualities' in
Proceedings of the Aristotelian Society suppl. vol., 1988.
[14] J. Dreier, 'Internalism and Speaker Relativism', *Ethics* 101 (1990). As Dreier himself
puts it: 'I have some sympathy for emotivism and other noncognitive meta-ethical theories.
Relativism flows naturally from them, and speaker relativism is in a way their child.' (p. 14)

The kind of relativism I advocate is roughly this: the content of a moral term in a context is a function of the affective attitudes of the speaker in the context. Thus, 'x is good' means 'x is highly evaluated by the standards of system M,' where M is filled in by looking at the affective or motivational states of the speaker and constructing from them a practical system.[15]

In deciding whether someone's claim that something is good is true we are thus to use the content of the speaker's affective or motivational states to construct a system of rules of evaluation, and then we are to measure the extent to which that thing accords with these rules. The sentence 'x is good', as uttered by the speaker, is true just in case x scores well, false otherwise.

The 'roughly' is important, however, for Dreier immediately goes on to qualify his analysis. The affective or motivational states of the speaker out of which we construct a practical system are not those the speaker actually has, but rather those she 'normally' has.[16] This qualification is made in response to examples, like those we have already considered, of agents who make moral judgements without being motivated: cases of addiction, alienation, depression, emotional disturbance and the like. In the sense in which Dreier uses the term 'normal', these are to be considered abnormal cases. Let's grant this for the time being.

Given his relativist account of the content of a moral belief Dreier gives the following explanation of internalism. Internalism tells us that agents who believe they morally ought to φ in circumstances C are either appropriately motivated or practically irrational. But when a speaker says that she morally ought to φ in C she describes φ-ing in C as meeting certain standards, standards which are determined by her motivations in the normal case. It therefore follows that, in the normal case, she will be appropriately motivated. Indeed, in the normal case, a speaker's judgement that she morally ought to φ in C will be *both* an expression of her belief that φ-ing in C is highly evaluated by her moral system *and* an expression of her desire to φ in C.

Dreier's explanation depends crucially on the idea of a normal condition. Though he admits he doesn't know how to specify this idea rigorously, he is confident that we do have an 'independent grip' on what normal conditions are, and that we will therefore not

[15] Dreier 'Internalism and Speaker Relativism', p. 9.
[16] Dreier, 'Internalism and Speaker Relativism' pp. 9–14.

be reduced to defining them as the 'circumstances under which a person is motivated by what she believes to be good'.[17] Unfortunately, however, the little he says about the independent grip we have is discouraging.

> It is clear to me that if everyone in a community behaves in a certain way, then that behaviour is normal in the community, and if a person has a certain state of character for all of her life, then behaviour flowing from that state is normal for her.[18]

According to Dreier 'everyone' and 'always' are thus supposed to imply 'normal'. Normality is thus a *statistical* matter. The real question is therefore whether a statistical conception of normality can play the role required in spelling out the content of a moral belief.

An agent's desires in normal conditions are supposed to fix the content of her moral system. But there seems to be no conceptual barrier to the idea of someone who lives the whole of her life in an alienated, depressed, or emotionally disturbed state – someone whose normal desires, given a statistical gloss on 'normal', for this reason run contrary to the content of both her moral beliefs and her moral system. And nor does there seem to be any conceptual barrier to the idea of an entire community of such agents. Yet there would have to be such conceptual barriers if the content of an agent's moral system, and so the content of her moral beliefs, were fixed by her desires in the normal case, as Dreier understands normality.

The fact that Dreier appeals to statistical notions in giving the cognitive content of a moral judgement undermines his explanation of internalism as well. The connection between moral belief and motivation posited by internalism is, after all, a normative connection. But because he appeals to a statistical conception of normality in explaining that connection, Dreier's theory entails that there is at best a 'generally speaking' or 'for the most part' connection – a connection which, even if it were in place, would be entirely lacking in normative significance.

It might be thought that these objections are superficial, and that Dreier could easily amend speaker relativism to overcome these difficulties.[19] But I want now to argue that this is not the case. My

---

[17] Dreier, 'Internalism and Speaker Relativism', p. 13.
[18] Dreier, 'Internalism and Speaker Relativism', p. 14.
[19] At one point Dreier suggests a sophistication of his theory which might be thought to address just these difficulties: 'I started by allowing the speaker's actual motivational states

argument for this conclusion requires only a very uncontroversial assumption: namely, that whatever account we give of the cognitive content of a moral judgement, that account must enable us to make sense of the distinction between justified and unjustified uses of coercive power. My argument is to be that speaker relativism undermines this uncontroversial assumption.

Imagine a conversation between two people, A and B. B says to A 'You morally ought to φ in C', and A replies 'It is not the case that I morally ought to φ in C'. Let's suppose further that this conversation takes place in a context in which B is in a position to coerce A, and that B says, by way of justifying his use of coercive power, 'I morally ought to force you to φ in C'. A denies this, saying 'You morally ought not to force me to φ in C'.

As described this conversation is, of course, abstract and schematic. But it does allow us to bring out a crucial point. At least as we ordinarily see things, if what B says is true then it follows that his use of coercive power over A is indeed justified, and that in turn must entail that B's use of coercive power can be conceptualized in a way that makes it seem very different from the power exercised by, say, a thug or a gangster. A gangster who holds a gun at his victim's head and demands 'Your money or your life' is *simply* forcing his will upon his victim against his victim's wishes. B, by contrast, is not simply forcing his will upon A against A's wishes, at least not if his use of coercive power is justified. Whatever account

---

to determine completely the relevant moral system. The modification in response to counterexamples to crude internalism allowed the moral system to be picked out by the speaker's motivations under normal conditions. The sophisticated relativist will look to what Westermark called the "retributive emotions". So elements of the system will be rules which are such that if the speaker violates them he will tend to feel guilty; if others violate them he will tend to feel indignation; and so forth.' ('Internalism and Speaker Relativism', p. 24) The ideas of guilt and indignation might be thought to introduce an appropriately normative element into the picture while allowing Dreier's basic idea to remain the same. According to this more sophisticated theory, when a speaker says that she morally ought to φ in C she is saying that φ-ing in C is highly evaluated by system M, where M is a system of rules whose content is filled in by looking at the causes of her feelings of guilt and indignation. The following principle is therefore analytic: if an agent believes that it is morally right to φ in C then either she is motivated to φ in C or she feels guilty. It might be thought that this principle is equivalent to the truth embodied in internalism. However, this more sophisticated theory is no improvement if, as it seems to me, feelings of guilt cannot be understood except as the feelings we have when we believe that we have done something wrong, for then the derived principle, which is supposed to be equivalent to internalism, is the following: if an agent believes she morally ought to φ in C then either she is motivated to φ in C or she has the feelings that accompany her belief that she has done the wrong thing. Since internalists and externalists can both accept this principle it is obviously not equivalent to internalism.

we give of the cognitive content of moral judgement, then, it must not turn out that cases of justified coercion – that is, cases like that described in which B's judgement that he morally ought to force A to φ in C are true – are not substantively different from cases involving a gangster and his victim. Unfortunately, however, this is just what happens if we accept speaker relativism.

Consider once again the abstract conversation just described. According to speaker relativism B says that A's φ-ing in C is highly evaluated by moral system M, where the content of M is determined by B's affective attitudes. A's reply is that it is not the case that A's φ-ing in C is highly evaluated by moral system M*, where the content of moral system M* is determined by A's affective attitudes. B insists that his forcing A to φ in C is highly evaluated by moral system M, where the content of M is determined by B's affective attitudes, and A's reply is, once again, that it is not the case that B's forcing A to φ in C is highly evaluated by moral system M*, where the content of moral system M* is determined by A's affective attitudes.

As should now be evident, however, A and B are, potentially at any rate, not even contradicting each other. A's talk is all about a moral system whose content is fixed by his, A's, affective attitudes, whereas B's is all about a moral system whose content is fixed by his, B's. It is therefore possible that B may even be brought to agree with A that it is not the case that A's φ-ing in C, and B's forcing A to φ in C, are highly evaluated by moral system M* where the content of M* is determined by A's affective attitudes, and that A may be brought to agree with B about how these acts are evaluated by moral system M. It is possible because, on speaker relativist assumptions, it is both a conceptual and an empirical possibility that A's and B's affective attitudes simply differ in crucial respects.

This is all deeply problematic, however, at least given the assumption that an analysis of the cognitive content of a moral judgement must allow us to preserve the commonsense distinction between justified and unjustified use of coercive power. For that distinction simply collapses under the speaker relativist's analysis. The gangster is supposed to be unjustified in his use of coercive power because he is *simply* forcing his will upon his victim against his victim's wishes. B's use of coercive power is supposed to be different, at least if his claim that he morally ought to force A to φ in C is true. But B's use of coercive power is not different – or not if we accept the speaker relativist's analysis of moral claims. The truth of B's claim that he morally ought to force A to φ in C requires just that B's forcing A to ϕ in C is highly evaluated by a moral system whose content is fixed by his, *B*'s, affective states, and, at least as I understand it, that is just a fancy way of saying that the truth of B's claim requires that B's will is to force A to ϕ in C. A's will on this issue is simply different from B's, just as the victim's wishes differ from the gangster's. A and B thus look for all the world, in relevant respects at any rate, like a victim and a gangster. Their wills simply conflict. The distinction between justified and unjustified use of coercive power has collapsed. Internalism's Wheel therefore turns again.

III Harman's Moral Relativism

We are now looking for a theory that can explain three things. First, it must give an account of what moral beliefs are beliefs about; second, it must use that account to explain the normative connection between moral belief and motivation; and third, it must use that account to explain the distinction between justified and unjustified uses of·coercive power. Speaker relativism is in fact closely related to another theory which does make some headway in this regard, Gilbert Harman's version of moral relativism.[20]

Harman begins by distinguishing 'inner judgements', judgements about what people ought to do, from 'outer' judgements, judgements to the effect that this or that person is evil. He then focuses on inner judgements, judgements of moral obligation, as opposed to outer judgements, evaluations of people's characters, in order to advance the following 'soberly logical thesis'. When we say of someone, A, that she morally ought to ϕ in certain circumstances C, Harman tells us that the logical form of what we say is best captured by treating 'ought' not as a three-place predicate – 'Ought (A, ϕ, C)' – as perhaps it seems, but rather as a four-place predicate – 'Ought (A, ϕ, C, M)'. What this means is, roughly, that given A has motivating attitudes M, attitudes shared by the speaker, and given that she is in circumstances C, ϕ-ing is the course of action for A that is supported by the best reasons.

In order better to understand Harman's analysis, and to see how it differs from Dreier's, we need to focus on which motivating attitudes he has in mind. He tells us he has in mind 'intentions to adhere to a particular agreement on the understanding that others also intend to do so', where the agreement is not supposed to be

[20] Harman, 'Moral Relativism Defended'.

an overt ritual or ceremony, but rather, as he puts it, simply an 'agreement in intentions'.[21]

> It is enough if various members of a society knowingly reach an agreement in intentions – each intending to act in certain ways on the understanding that the others have similar intentions.

Moreover, as he immediately concedes, the precise content of these intentions may be difficult to specify. Such intentions may 'in various ways be inconsistent, incoherent, or self-defeating'.[22] But this too he thinks his analysis can easily accommodate.

> Moral reasoning is a form of practical reasoning. One begins with certain beliefs and intentions, including intentions that are part of one's acceptance of the moral understanding in a given group. In reasoning, one modifies one's intentions, often by forming new intentions, sometimes by giving up old ones, so that one's plans become more rational and coherent – or, rather, one seeks to make all of one's attitudes coherent with each other.[23]

When Harman says that 'ought' judgements are made relative to a set of motivating attitudes, he therefore seems to have in mind those intentions to act in certain ways, on the understanding that others also have such intentions, that are part of the set of intentions that the speaker and the agent in question would have if their intentions and other attitudes formed a maximally coherent and rational set.[24]

Let me digress for a moment. Harman labels this a set of 'intentions', but the label seems quite inappropriate. His basic idea is that a speaker's claim that an agent A morally ought to φ in C is

---

[21] Harman, 'Moral Relativism Defended', p. 13

[22] Harman, 'Moral Relativism Defended', p. 16

[23] Harman, 'Moral Relativism Defended', p. 20.

[24] Let me here acknowledge that my interpretation of Harman goes beyond anything he explicitly says in the text. I assume, perhaps wrongly, that Harman thinks that once I have engaged in a process of moral reasoning I am still able to make judgements about what my earlier, less coherent, self morally ought to have done, because both my earlier, less coherent, self and my later, more coherent, self make moral judgements relative to the same set of intentions: namely, the maximally coherent and rational set. An alternative view is that we always make moral judgements relative to the intentions we in fact have. The drawback of this alternative is that, once I have engaged in a process of moral reasoning, I may be unable to make judgements about what my earlier, less coherent, self morally ought to have done. This will be the case if the process of reasoning has led me to adopt different intentions. My interpretation of Harman thus has the virtue of making moral reasoning a means by which we can adopt a critical perspective on our less coherent and rational selves, a means by which we can discover what we morally ought to have done.

made true, if it is true, by the fact that both the speaker and A would have a pro-attitude – as I would prefer to call it – towards A's φ-ing in C if they had a maximally coherent and rational set of pro-attitudes, each on the understanding that the other would have similar pro-attitudes (from now on I will omit this qualification). Let's call the possible world in which the speaker and A have a maximally coherent and rational set of pro-attitudes the 'evaluating world', and the possible world in which A is in circumstances C, the possible world that both the speaker and A are evaluating, the 'evaluated world'.[25] We can then restate Harman's basic idea as follows. A speaker's claim that an agent A morally ought to φ in C is made true, if it is true, by the fact that the speaker and A *in the evaluating world* each have a pro-attitude towards A's φ-ing in C *in the evaluated world*. If this is right, however, then it should be clear that these pro-attitudes are not properly labelled 'intentions' at all, at least not if an agent's intentions are psychological states that are crucially concerned with her own possibilities for action. For there is no necessity that the pro-attitudes the speaker and A have in the evaluating world, the world in which they are maximally rational, about what is to be done in the evaluated world, the world in which A is in circumstances C, have any connection at all with their own possibilities for action in the evaluating possible world. Their intentions in the evaluating world are, after all, a function of their view of their own circumstances, circumstances they face in the evaluating world. But the circumstances A faces in the evaluated world may be completely different. From now on I will therefore omit any mention of intentions in describing Harman's view. I will say, instead, that as he sees things, the truth of moral claims is relative to shared pro-attitudes. Here ends the digression.

Harman's version of moral relativism differs from Dreier's in several key respects. First, though Harman, like Dreier, makes a speaker's own pro-attitudes part of the truth conditions of her claims about what other agents morally ought to do, the pro-attitudes in question are not those the speaker normally has, where 'normality' is a statistical matter, but rather those that she would have if she were to come up with a maximally coherent and rational set of such attitudes. Harman thus explicitly defines 'morally ought' in normative terms, for the attitudes agents would have if they were maximally coherent and rational are those they

---

[25] For a futher development of this idea see my 'Internal Reasons', *Philosophy and Phenomenological Research* 55 (1995).

82   MICHAEL SMITH

rationally should have. Second, in striking opposition to Dreier's speaker relativism, Harman also makes the pro-attitudes of those about whom a speaker is speaking part of the truth conditions of a speaker's claims about what people morally ought to do. The first difference is crucial for the explanation Harman can give of internalism. The second is crucial for the account he can give of the distinction between justified and unjustified uses of coercive power.

Consider the explanation of internalism. If an agent believes that she would have a pro-attitude towards φ-ing in C if she had a maximally coherent and rational set of pro-attitudes then she does indeed seem practically irrational if she doesn't actually have a pro-attitude towards φ-ing in C. Coherence is, after all, on the side of psychologies that combine an agent's believing that she would have a pro-attitude towards φ-ing in C if she had a maximally coherent and rational set of pro-attitudes with her actually having a pro-attitude towards φ-ing in C, rather than psychologies that include that belief but lack the corresponding pro-attitude. Agents whose psychologies evolve in accordance with a tendency towards coherence, then, will tend to be moved in accordance with their moral beliefs. In this way Harman's theory can explain the requisite normative connection between moral belief and motivation. Agents who have moral beliefs but lack corresponding motivations exhibit a kind of incoherence in their overall psychological state. This seems to me to be an eminently plausible explanation of internalism.[26]

Consider now the distinction between justified and unjustified uses of coercive power. Suppose B says that he morally ought to force A to φ in C, and that A denies this, saying that it is not the case that B morally ought to force him to φ in C. The question on which the justification of B's use of coercive power is supposed to turn is which of A's and B's opinions are true, which mistaken. And this is indeed the case, given Harman's analysis. If A's belief that it is not the case that B morally ought to force her to φ in C is mistaken, and the right thing for A to believe is that B morally ought to force her to φ in C, then it must be the case that both A and B would share the very same pro-attitudes towards B's use of coercive power if they had a maximally coherent and rational set of such attitudes. There is therefore a relatively straightforward sense in which B's use of coercive power against A is not merely a matter of B forcing his will on A, for his use of coercive power is

[26] See also my 'Internal Reasons'.

also, in a sense, a matter of his forcing A's will upon A. B is simply doing what A would want done to himself if he, A, had a maximally coherent and rational set of pro-attitudes. As with the explanation of internalism, this seems to me an eminently plausible explanation of the difference between justified and unjustified uses of coercive power.

Have we therefore found the theory we have been looking for? Unfortunately we have not, for we have so far failed to discuss a crucial part of Harman's theory: the theory of outer moral judgements. When I said at the beginning that Harman distinguishes inner from outer judgements I didn't explain what outer judgements were, I simply gave his example: judgements to the effect that someone or other is evil. Now that we have his theory of inner moral judgements before us, however, the difference between inner and outer moral judgements is easy to explain.

A moral judgement made by a speaker about another person whose truth requires certain pro- and con-attitudes on the part of both the speaker and the person spoken of is, according to Harman, an *inner* moral judgement. Harman thinks that all claims about what people morally ought to do are inner judgements. But a moral judgement made by a speaker about another person whose truth requires no such attitudes on the part of the person spoken of is an *outer* moral judgement. Harman tells us that claims to the effect that this person or that is evil are outer judgements. Roughly speaking, then, judgements of moral obligation are inner judgements, character assessments are outer judgements.

Harman illustrates the need for a theory of outer moral judgements by considering what we can legitimately say about Adolph Hitler. According to Harman Hitler was beyond the 'motivational reach' of the moral considerations we use to condemn him.[27] Given Harman's theory of inner judgements it is literally false to say of Hitler that he did what he morally ought not to have done when he ordered the extermination of the Jews. It is false because it is not the case that Hitler, like us, would have had a con-attitude towards his doing so if he had had a maximally coherent and rational set of such attitudes. The true claims Hitler could make about his moral obligations may therefore be completely different from the true claims we could make about ours. This is why Harman calls his theory a form of moral relativism. However, despite the fact he thinks this form of moral relativism is true,

[27] Harman, 'Moral Relativism Defended', p. 8.

Harman insists that we can and do rightly condemn Hitler on moral grounds. This is because we can and do rightly say of Hitler that he is evil, where the truth of this claim requires nothing from a maximally coherent and rational Hitler in the way of suitable pro- or con-attitudes.

Harman thus adds a theory of outer judgements to his theory of inner judgements because of the inherent *limits* of the latter. But is the theory of outer judgements plausible? I do not think so. For one thing, it forces us to suppose that various logical relations which we would ordinarily suppose to hold between inner and outer judgements fail to hold. For example, we would ordinarily suppose that 'A is evil' entails 'A is disposed reliably to do what A morally ought not to do', that this is true simply in virtue of the meanings of the words used. But Harman's theory tells us that the entailment is fallacious. Hitler may be evil even though he is not disposed to do what he morally ought not to do, as the first requires less for its truth than the second. Yet what would be our reason for supposing someone is evil, if not that he is disposed reliably to do what he morally ought not to do? A theory that provides uniform truth conditions for inner and outer judgements therefore seems preferable to a theory like Harman's that provides different truth conditions.[28]

Worse still, Harman's theory of outer moral judgements cannot play the role it needs to play in his overall theory of morality. Its role is to provide a set of moral judgements we can legitimately make about people, like Hitler, about whom we cannot legitimately make inner moral judgements. But why do we need to be able to make such judgements? We need to be able to make such judgements in order to be able to condemn their behaviour on moral grounds, so justifying our stand against them and, ultimately, our use of coercive power. But precisely because outer judgements differ from inner moral judgements in the way they do, we are

---

[28] Here I find myself in agreement with David Brink: 'This distinction between inner and outer judgements may seem somewhat puzzling. If morality's practical or action-guiding character establishes a connection between moral considerations and reasons for action, shouldn't we expect all moral judgements to imply the existence of reasons for action? Are character assessments any less "inner" than ascriptions of obligation? . . . Indeed, Harman's distinction is incoherent if it should turn out that moral properties of character can be specified in terms of the relation between an agent's character and the fulfillment or failure to fulfill different obligations that the agent has.' Brink, 'Moral Realism Defended', in L. Pojman (ed.), *Ethical Theory: Classical and Contemporary Readings* (Belmont, CA: Wadsworth Publishing Company, 1989), p. 44.

unable even to make a coherent distinction between justified and unjustified use of coercive power simply in their terms.

Imagine trying to justify our use of coercion against Hitler by claiming that he is evil. What makes this claim true, if it is true, according to Harman? Presumably this claim has the same truth condition as a claim about what people morally ought to do *minus* the requirement that the person spoken of shares our pro-attitudes. Here we resort to a theory more like speaker relativism. We coerce Hitler because, as we see things, coercion is in accordance with the maximally coherent and rational set of pro-attitudes we would have. Hitler resists because, as he sees things, the extermination of the Jews is in accordance with the maximally coherent and rational set of attitudes he would have. Since, by Harman's lights, there is no sense in which either of us may suppose that our attitudes are rationally preferable to the other's, our justifiably coercing Hitler collapses, under analysis, into a case of our forcing our (maximally coherent and rational) will upon Hitler against his (maximally coherent and rational) wishes. Coercion justified by outer moral judgements therefore looks, in relevant respects at any rate, just like unjustified coercion.

Harman's moral relativism must therefore be rejected. His theory does, however, suggest how further progress might be made. Harman adds a theory of outer judgements to his theory of inner judgements because of what he perceives to be the inherent *limits* of the latter. As he sees things it is a conceptual truth that we are only able to make inner judgements about those whose maximally coherent and rational attitudes would be similar to our own. This seems right. But he also thinks that, as a matter of fact, different people's maximally coherent and rational sets of attitudes would all too often be very different from each other. This means that we will sometimes be unable to make inner judgements by way of criticizing the behaviour of those we want to criticize. However, granting the conceptual point, we should question the relevance of his empirical claim. Our task is to give an account of what moral beliefs are beliefs about. Surely the only relevant issue is therefore whether, when we make moral judgements, we in effect *presuppose* that we would all end up with the same pro- and con-attitudes if we each had a maximally coherent and rational set of such attitudes. The truth of this presupposition is neither here nor there. Internalism's Wheel therefore turns yet again, this time to a theory according to which we make just this presupposition.

IV The Non-Relative Version of the Dispositional Theory of Value

The non-relative version of the dispositional theory of value holds that claims about moral obligations and character assessments alike require that we would all of us converge upon the same set of pro- and con-attitudes if we each came up with a maximally coherent and rational set of such attitudes.[29] According to this theory all the moral judgements we ever make are therefore inner judgements. To say that we morally ought to φ in circumstances C requires that we would all of us have suitable pro-attitudes towards φ-ing in C if we had a maximally coherent and rational set of pro- and con-attitudes, and character assessments require a convergence in maximally coherent and rational attitudes as well because, according to this view, they are analysable in terms of judgements of moral obligation: to say that someone is evil is to say, *inter alia*, that he is disposed reliably to do what he morally ought not to do.

Unlike Harman's moral relativism the dispositional theory is therefore a non-relativist moral theory. It is non-relativist because the effect of the convergence requirement is to ensure that the truth of moral claims is independent of the peculiar pro- and con-attitudes of both those who make such claims and those about whom such claims are made. This is crucial for the explanation the theory is able to give of the distinction between justified and unjustified uses of coercive power. Thus, to take Harman's example, even though Hitler may have a con-attitude towards our preventing him from exterminating the Jews, and even though he may believe that this attitude would survive in a maximally coherent and rational set of such attitudes, in supposing that he morally ought not to do so we assume that his beliefs are false. When we coerce Hitler we therefore take ourselves not simply to be forcing our own maximally coherent and rational wills upon him against his maximally coherent and rational wishes, we take ourselves also to be forcing his own maximally coherent and rational will upon himself. Justifiably coercing Hitler thus does not collapse, under analysis, into a mere clash of wills.

The non-relative version of the dispositional theory of value offers us a straightforward explanation of the truth of internalism as well. Indeed, its explanation is the same as that made available by

[29] Smith, *The Moral Problem*, especially chs. 5 and 6. Other versions of the theory are defended by D. Lewis and M. Johnston in their contributions to the 'Dispositional Theories of Value' symposium in *Proceedings of the Aristotelian Society* suppl. vol., 1989.

Harman's theory. Internalism is true because coherence is on the side of psychologies that combine an agent's believing that she would have a pro-attitude towards φ-ing in C, if she had the maximally coherent and rational set of pro- and con-attitudes all agents would converge upon, with actually having a pro-attitude towards φ-ing in C, rather than on the side of psychologies that include that belief but lack the corresponding pro-attitude. A mismatch between moral belief and motivation is therefore a kind of incoherence.

The non-relative version of the dispositional theory of value thus seems to explain the three things we want explained: it gives us an account of the cognitive content of a moral judgement, it uses that account to explain the normative connection between moral belief and motivation, and it uses that account to make a coherent distinction between justified and unjustified uses of coercive power. The theory pays a significant price for these explanations, however. For note how strong the convergence requirement really is.

The truth of the claim that we morally ought to φ in C requires that we would all of us have a pro-attitude towards φ-ing in C, if we had a maximally coherent and rational set of pro- and con-attitudes, not merely *contingently*, but *necessarily*. The convergence requirement must be understood in this way because a weaker, contingent, convergence requirement, which entails simply that:

1. In the actual world we would all have maximally coherent and rational sets of pro- and con-attitudes with the same content, the content of our moral obligations, but there is another possible world in which different agents have maximally coherent and rational sets of pro- and con-attitudes with different content.

is simply inconsistent with two further claims, claims we cannot reject, namely:

2. There is a combined possible world that contains both us as we actually are and them as they are in their world.

and

3. It is coherent to suppose that we would be justified in coercing them in the combined possible world.

This set is inconsistent because, as we have seen, the very coherence of the distinction between justified and unjustified uses of coercive power requires that the parties involved would each have attitudes with the same content if they had maximally coherent and rational sets of attitudes. Only so can the justified use coercive power be a matter of inflicting the coerced's own will upon them. The truth of (1) and (2) would therefore undermine the truth of (3). It follows that we must therefore reject (1). The convergence requirement must be necessary, not merely contingent.

According to the dispositional theory, then, in making moral judgements we presuppose that, *necessarily*, if we had a maximally coherent and rational set of pro- and con-attitudes we would all have attitudes with the same content. Of course, the dispositional theory is simply an analysis of the cognitive content of a moral judgement. It tells us what would have to be the case for moral claims to be true, it does not tell us whether any such claims are true. The theory is therefore consistent with an *error theory* of moral judgement, consistent with the claim that moral judgements are all based on a *false* presupposition: namely, that we would all converge on the same set of pro- and con-attitudes if we had maximally coherent and rational sets of such attitudes.[30] But a dilemma now looms large.

On the first horn the concepts of 'maximal coherence' and 'rationality' are given their ordinary everyday meaning. But then the objection is that it is simply implausible to suppose that something so obviously false – namely, that we would all have attitudes with the same content if we had maximally coherent and rational sets of pro- and con-attitudes – could be presupposed not just to be true, but necessarily true, by everyone who makes moral judgements. Think again about Hitler. Isn't it just obvious that he would not have the same attitudes as us if we both had maximally coherent and rational sets of attitudes? If so then it is implausible to suppose, as the dispositional theory supposes, that ordinary folk, when they moralise about Hitler, make the utterly preposterous presupposition that he would.

On the other horn of the dilemma the plausibility of the presupposition is granted, but only because it is assumed that we further presuppose something capable of explaining its truth: specifically, that a set of pro- and con-attitudes counts as maximally coherent and rational only if they are pro- and con-attitudes had towards doing what morally ought and ought not to be done respectively. But if this is part of what we presuppose in presupposing that there would be a necessary convergence in our maximally coherent and rational sets of pro- and con-attitudes then

---

[30] Compare Mackie, *Ethics*, ch. 1.

the non-relative version of the dispositional theory of value has clearly been abandoned. Facts about our moral obligations are being thought of as independent, thus far unanalyzed, facts. In order to have a theory that is credible at all, then, it seems that we must abandon the dispositional theory and look for an account of the cognitive content of moral judgements which posits independent facts about our moral obligations. Internalism's Wheel therefore turns to such a theory.

V Moral Platonism

Moral platonism is the view of moral facts John Mackie ascribes to common sense in his *Ethics: Inventing Right and Wrong*. According to this view, the concept of a moral feature is the concept of an 'objectively prescriptive' feature of acts and characters.[31] These features are prescriptive in that it is part of their nature to elicit desire from those who recognize them. They are objective in that they elude analysis in subjective terms. Moral claims are not made true by facts about speakers or those spoken of, in the manner of Dreier's or Harman's theories. Nor are they made true by facts about rational creatures as such in the manner of the non-relative version of the dispositional theory of value. They are made true by independent moral facts.

Let's grant, for the time being, the coherence of the moral platonist's conception of moral facts as objectively prescriptive features. Once we grant him this, he can explain the truth of internalism: internalism is true because of what it means to say that a moral belief is a belief about a 'prescriptive' feature of the world. He can also explain the coherence of the distinction between justified and unjustified uses of coercive power: coercion is justified whenever it is morally obligatory, where being morally obligatory is an objectively prescriptive feature of an act of coercion, a feature that eludes analysis in subjective terms; being justified thus does not reduce, under analysis, to facts about anyone's will. And, finally, he can explain the necessary convergence in maximally coherent and rational sets of pro- and con-attitudes: such attitudes converge because they are, by definition, formed in response to the objectively prescriptive features of things. The real question we must address is therefore whether we should grant the platonist the coherence of his conception of moral facts.

---

[31] Mackie, *Ethics*, p. 35.

Consider the platonist's idea that moral features are objective. Moral claims are not supposed to be made true by facts about speakers or those spoken of, in the manner of Dreier's or Harman's theories, and nor are they supposed to be made true by facts about the pro- and con-attitudes of maximally coherent and rational creatures either, in the manner of the non-relative version of the dispositional theory of value. Moral facts are independent facts, facts that elude analysis in subjective terms. The platonist therefore seems to be conceiving of moral facts in the way in which many philosophers suppose we might conceive of *primary* qualities, as opposed to *secondary* qualities.[32] However, as John McDowell points out, it is difficult to square the idea that moral facts are objective in this sense with the idea that they are also prescriptive.

> For it seems impossible – at least on reflection – to take seriously the idea of something that is like a primary quality in being simply there, independently of human sensibility, but is nevertheless intrinsically (not conditionally on the contingencies of human sensibility) such as to elicit some 'attitude' or state of will from someone who becomes aware of it.[33]

Indeed, the idea of an objectively prescriptive feature looks like a contradiction. Insofar as they are objective they must be conceived of independently of any effects they might have upon rational agents. But insofar as they are prescriptive they must be conceived of in terms of a very particular effect they have upon rational agents: namely, their impact upon a rational agent's pro-attitudes.[34]

Worse still, the idea that moral features might be objective and independent of facts about human subjects in the sense in which the primary qualities of objects are objective and independent of facts about human subjects sits best with a *causal* model of moral knowledge, an account according to which moral knowledge is perceptual, or a matter of inference to the best scientific explanation, with moral facts playing a crucial causal role in the generation of that knowledge. But moral knowledge – or, at any rate, knowledge of fundamental moral truths or general principles – is a

[32] See especially C. McGinn, *The Subjective View* (Oxford: Clarendon Press, 1983), ch. 2.
[33] J. McDowell, 'Values and Secondary Qualities' in T. Honderich (ed.), *Morality and Objectivity* (London: Routledge and Kegan Paul, 1985), p. 111.
[34] M. Smith, 'Objectivity and Moral Realism: On the Significance of the Phenomenology of Moral Experience', in Haldane and Wright, p. 237.

relatively *a priori* matter, and, however we are to conceive of *a priori* knowledge in general, it seems quite inappropriate to suppose that we gain such knowledge via causal contact with the *a priori* truths. If this is right, however – that is, if the platonist is not entitled to say that moral facts are independent of rational agents in the sense of being the cause of moral knowledge in the manner of primary qualities – then it simply isn't clear how he is to give an account of the sense in which he takes moral facts to be independent of facts about human subjects. His account of independence loses all content.

We must therefore conclude that the moral platonist's conception of moral facts is indeed incoherent. And there is worse to come. For moral platonism is simply the latest in a series of theories all which have tried, and failed, to give an account of what moral beliefs are beliefs about. These theories form a spectrum, from the extreme subjectivism of speaker relativism to the equally extreme objectivism of moral platonism. What should we conclude from the fact that they all fail? Many would have us draw the conclusion that moral judgements do not express moral beliefs at all. According to these theorists we should suppose instead that moral judgements express a psychological state of a kind more suited to entering into a direct explanation of the truth that lies in internalism: an emotion, or a feeling, or a desire. Internalism's Wheel therefore turns once more, or so they tell us. But, as our discussion makes plain, if we were to embrace this conclusion we would simply be arguing ourselves around in a circle. We would be led back to expressivism, and then on around Internalism's Wheel once more. Perhaps we should therefore draw the more pessimistic conclusion that the very idea of a moral judgement is incoherent. Or perhaps not.

VI Reassessment

Have the objections to the various theories really been as forceful as they have been portrayed to be? I do not think so. The weakest, as I see it, is the objection to the non-relative version of the dispositional theory of value, the view that we morally ought to ϕ in C just in case we would all of us converge, and necessarily so, upon a desire that we ϕ in C if we had a maximally coherent and rational set of pro- and con-attitudes. The objection takes the form of a dilemma. Either the concepts of maximal coherence and rationality are given their ordinary everyday meanings, in which case it is simply incredible to suppose that anyone would ever make moral judgements, presupposing as they do such a manifest falsehood, or else these concepts are to be defined in terms of independent facts about moral obligations, in which case we have to abandon the dispositional theory in favour of moral platonism. But as I see it neither horn of the dilemma does justice to our ordinary concepts of coherence and rationality. There is a third alternative in between.

In order to find out what our moral obligations are, let's agree that we initially have no alternative but to consider what we would all end up having pro- and con-attitudes towards insofar as our sets of pro- and con-attitudes come closer to maximal coherence and rationality in the most uncontroversial sense of these terms. But then, in order to find out whether one or another of us has a maximally coherent and rational set of pro- and con-attitudes, in the fullest possible sense, let's agree that we initially have no choice but to consider whether one or another of us has a set of attitudes that have, as their content, our moral obligations, as we ordinarily take them to be. There is no contradiction here. Rather we should conclude that neither concept, neither maximal coherence and rationality on the one hand nor moral obligation on the other, can be wholly understood except in terms of the other. Our ordinary, everyday, concepts of maximal coherence and rationality, and moral obligation, must rather be *inter-defined*.

On this way of seeing things the task before us, in coming up with a complete account of the cognitive content of a moral judgement, is thus to see whether we can extend our most uncontroversial ways of understanding of coherence and rationality so as to make plausible the idea that maximally coherent and rational creatures, as we newly understand these notions, would all converge upon a set of pro-attitudes towards their moral obligations. And this task in turn requires that we amend and precisify, wherever necessary, our ordinary everyday understanding of what our moral obligations are so as to bring our moral obligations more in line with the sorts of pro- and con-attitudes we would have if we had a maximally coherent and rational set, as these are newly understood.[35]

The fact that we need to play these two ideas off against each other in this way, that neither concept can be wholly understood except in terms of the other, means that in moral philosophy there

---

[35] The idea should sound familiar from J. Rawls, 'Outline of a Decision Procedure for Ethics', *Philosophical Review* 50 (1951).

is no clear line to be drawn between the tasks of conceptual analysis and substantive moral theorising. And indeed, as partial confirmation of this idea, note that it is in terms of such a play-off between the two ideas of a maximally coherent and rational set of pro- and con-attitudes on the one hand, and a moral obligation on the other, that we can perhaps best understand the appeal of many of the devices employed in contemporary normative ethics: the ideal observer,[36] the veil of ignorance,[37] the role-reversal test,[38] the agreements of idealised contractors,[39] and the like. For these devices can each be seen as different ways of giving content to the idea that our moral obligations derive from a procedure whereby we rationally justify our desires, where that procedure in turn aims to capture or model our susceptibility as rational creatures to the legitimate claims made against us by others, given a suitable characterisation of 'legitimate'.

Of course, as perhaps these examples make plain, no attempt to enrich our understanding of our concepts of coherence and rationality so as to make plausible the idea that we would all converge upon a set of pro-attitudes towards our moral obligations if we had a maximally coherent and rational set of such attitudes is guaranteed to succeed. The devices described are all controversial as interpretations of rationality, and, in some cases at least, indeterminate in the substantive conclusions they deliver. Indeed, there is no guarantee that any such attempt will succeed. But that is simply to reiterate the point that the dispositional theory, even if it is cast in a non-reductive mould in the way I am suggesting, leaves open the possibility of an error theory. Our concepts of a maximally coherent and rational set of pro- and con-attitudes on the one hand, and a moral obligation on the other, may resist being brought into equilibrium with each other. But, if they do, then the right conclusion to draw is that neither of these concepts makes any real sense. Showing that this is so would, however, be an enormous task. In effect it would require showing that no progress can be made in normative ethics.

A complete defence of the suggestion I am making here would

---

[36] R. Firth, 'Ethical Absolutism and the Ideal Observer', *Philosophy and Phenomenological Research* 12 (1952).

[37] J. Rawls, *A Theory of Justice* (Cambridge MA: Harvard University Press, 1971), Part 1.

[38] R. M. Hare, 'Ethical Theory and Utilitarianism', in A. Sen and B. Williams (eds.), *Utilitarianism and Beyond* (Cambridge: Cambridge University Press, 1982).

[39] Harman, 'Moral Relativism Defended'; T. M. Scanlon, 'Contractualism and Utilitarianism', in Sen and Williams.

require more in the way of argument. We would need to show, at the very least, that the project of conceptual analysis does not itself force us to take a reductive, as opposed to a non-reductive, route. Providing these further arguments would, however, take us way beyond the scope of the present paper. I here simply assume that these arguments can be provided.[40] But once we clear the way for non-reductive analyses of the kind envisaged, and help ourselves to analyses of moral obligation in terms of rationality and rationality in terms of moral obligation, it should be clear that the dispositional theorist can avoid the dilemma foisted upon him by the moral platonist. The platonist is right to insist that reduction is implausible, but wrong to suppose that the alternative to reduction is to conceive of moral facts as wholly independent of our maximally coherent and rational attitudes.

Somewhat tentatively, then, my conclusion is that the non-reductive, non-relative version of the dispositional theory of value provides a stable stopping point for Internalism's Wheel. That is good news for internalists, of course. But it should also be good news for those interested in substantive moral issues as well. For even though, as we have seen, the theory is so far consistent with the possibility of an error theory, it does at least tell us the task we must undertake if we are to show that the error theory is mistaken, and the task it tells us to undertake looks by no means to be impossible. Indeed, it looks to be the same as the task of substantive moral theorising itself.[41]

Philosophy Program
Research School of Social Sciences
Australian National University
Canberra, ACT, 0200
Australia
email: msmith@coombs.anu.edu.au

---

[40] I attempt to provide these arguments in *The Moral Problem*, ch. 2.
[41] Thanks to John O'Leary-Hawthorne and Brad Hooker for helpful comments.

INDEX